MW00737465

THE
POISON OF
POLITICS

7/7/11

claire—

I can't put into words
how appreciative I am that you
purchased my book.. Thank you!
I hope you enjoy the read. May
you have continued good fortune.

THE
POISON OF
POLITICS

REX REED

TATE PUBLISHING & Enterprises

The Poison of Politics
Copyright © 2010 by Rex Reed. All rights reserved.

No part of this publication may be reproduced, stored in a retrieval system or transmitted in any way by any means, electronic, mechanical, photocopy, recording or otherwise without the prior permission of the author except as provided by USA copyright law.

The opinions expressed by the author are not necessarily those of Tate Publishing, LLC.

Published by Tate Publishing & Enterprises, LLC
127 E. Trade Center Terrace | Mustang, Oklahoma 73064 USA
1.888.361.9473 | www.tatepublishing.com

Tate Publishing is committed to excellence in the publishing industry. The company reflects the philosophy established by the founders, based on Psalm 68:11, *"The Lord gave the word and great was the company of those who published it."*

Book design copyright © 2010 by Tate Publishing, LLC. All rights reserved.
Cover design by Kristen Verser
Interior design by Stefanie Rane

Published in the United States of America

ISBN: 978-1-61663-653-1
1. Political Science, Political Ideologies, Conservatism & Liberalism
2. Political Science, Political Process, General
10.10.08

TO GOD IS ALL THE GLORY.

TABLE OF CONTENTS

9   **Preface**

16   By the People, For the People

27   Fannie Mae, Freddie Mac and
Politicians as Experts on the Economy

43   **Political Discourse**

49   Terror Attack, War and Responsibility

60   Fannie and Freddie Revisited;
Character of Those in the Know

69   Politicians, People, Media: Some Issues

91   **Social Observations**

110   Lips Can Stop Very Little for Good or Ill

119   Government by Liberals, for Liberals

134 Freedom and English

157 Liberal Policies, Racial Challenges
and the Importance of Education

**179 Role, Purpose, and Power
of Government**

200 Success or Failure

223 Wait, what?

231 Epilogue

233 Endnotes

PREFACE

I must admit that I do not necessarily have singular expertise or experience that uniquely qualifies me to be the author of a book; however, I consider myself as qualified as anyone else to evaluate the political landscape of our country thanks, in part to a degree in Political Science and personal observations throughout the course of my life.

For those who had the privilege of witnessing the presidential campaign and subsequent election of 2008, there seemed to be plenty of people in the country for whom expertise or experience was evidently not that significant. I suppose I now have something in common with the forty-fourth president besides the fact that we are both men. His lack of expertise and experience was painfully obvious during the prolonged campaign, though I must give him credit for his ability to influence the masses given where that talent has taken him. And I can only hope my success mirrors the success he enjoyed as a candidate.

My task to become a published author does not necessarily equate to Mr. Obama's accomplishment as President of the United States! By writing this book, I have done what I believe is necessary to ensure that America continues to be the greatest country on the face of the earth. By virtue of the fact that I am an American citizen with rights granted by our founding documents qualifies me to say what I have said in this book. And I cannot thank each of you enough for supporting my efforts.

Actually, my initial motivation for writing this book can be attributed to some who have been elected to represent "we the people." Many politicians have lost touch with reality, and have in many cases dismissed the Constitution. Perhaps, if our way of life was not as threatened as it now is, I may not have been so compelled to have written this book to begin with. Actually, I do not consider it compulsory to write about freedom, liberty, equality, and accountability because I do not believe that such words are mere sound bites to enhance a political speech. I attribute additional impetus for writing this book to my wife, Margaret, who continues to be a source of encouragement, strength, and confidence in my life, without whom, this project would not have been realized. I cannot adequately express thanks enough for her that would remotely begin to justify my respect and affection for her.

I consider myself to be a student of the Constitution, Declaration of Independence, and our form of government in general; in fact, I prefer the designation of student as it relates to these profound documents. Too often self-described scholars, or those to whom this label is given, have become impervious to a viewpoint that is contrary to their own. I am certain that anyone who knows me, even remotely, does not consider me to be a scholar with regard to the Founding Documents of our country, and that is perfectly fine with me. I respect those who have risen to a scholarly pinnacle because that leaves more room for students like me. Besides, I believe a student is more apt to maintain a measure of humility and a hunger to learn, a characteristic desperately needed for one to continue the process of education.

Sometimes in our society we think we have arrived regarding our education; that we have achieved a level that is sufficient for the justification of haughty behavior toward those who are presumably "less educated" than ourselves. I think we have all witnessed our share of "scholars" who, when opening their mouths, appear to be anything but scholarly about the topic for which they are considered scholars, not because they lack knowledge or understanding about their topic of expertise, but because of their appalling lack of meekness. It seems that the more educated in our society should be the most humble, exhibiting profound gratitude for the opportunity to enhance intelligence.

Like many of you, I belong to that silent majority that is like an over-inflated balloon; as long as the balloon is left alone and admired, it will maintain its current shape, but if it goes near any type of penetrating object, it is in danger of being popped. Much has happened over the last few election cycles that have given us cause to be worried that the balloon is about to lose its blissful nature. Some elected politicians in our government have strayed from the principles that have made America the greatest nation on the planet; namely government for the people and by the people. My objective for writing this book is to point out some of the instances where those who hold elected office, among others, have abused authority that was not bestowed upon them at birth, but rather, given to them by "we the people."

The United States of America must always be a government for the people. Much has transpired in recent times that have led me to rehearse a phrase uttered by our forbearers at a time when they were struggling to escape the grasps of a powerful monarchy. As part of the "Declaration and Resolves" of the First Continental Congress in 1774, it was said regarding the unlawful dominance of the British that "To these grievous acts and measures, Americans cannot submit … " While the Colonists struggled to break free from the grips of power, they ultimately fought a war so that their independence might be preserved.

The enemy that we face today is more subtle and cunning than a people staring down the barrel of a British soldier's rifle; it is an enemy that resides within our nation and occupies the seats of government in the highest offices of the land. In order to maintain our God-given rights, we must be willing to defeat the enemies of freedom wherever they are found. I am advocating that "we the people," through lawful and dignified means, do all we can to secure the rights of the Declaration of Independence and constitutional liberties to ensure all the attendant blessings that are a consequence of such documents.

I am abundantly thankful for all who will take the time to read this book. Each of you is instrumental in helping me to fulfill a dream. The intimidating aspect from my perspective about writing this book is that you are at the mercy of my every indulgence. I have been given a new and incredibly different perspective as an author by being on the other side of the words, so to speak. As a reader, it is easy to play "Monday morning quarterback" and ruthlessly critique everything we read. I guess what I am trying to say is a profound "thank you" for all who actually take the time to contemplate the words contained within these pages. Remember, it is impossible for me to be upset with any of you considering my status as a pupil. It is my hope to be able to assist anyone taking the time to read this book to enjoy it and stay calm but resolute in the face of such gross misuse of authority by those occupying positions granted to them by the people. I know it is sometimes difficult to maintain a proper balance when dealing with some who have been elected to represent us.

Since her initial concurrence, Margaret has offered valuable suggestions and guidance throughout the process of writing. I am confident that this book will be successful because I am convinced that there are enough of us who want to see those in government do the right thing to ensure that our rights are preserved, instead of being concerned about the preservation of their power-grabbing agendas. I must, however, give credit for the success of this book to all the many wonderful politicians and members of the media, on whose words I have shamelessly taken a most wonderful journey because of all the incredible material from which I had to choose.

I take full responsibility for every word in this book. If there are errors or mistakes in grammar and punctuation, I am to blame. I owe great thanks to Tate Publishing for having the faith to accept this project, and for the work they have accomplished to bring this book to light. I have taken the time to research quotes to make sure that they accurately portray events. I am not about to pull the kinds of stunts like many of the politicians I write about by not accepting responsibility for my actions. As with everything good in my life, I give the glory and praise to God, without whom, nothing is possible.

I will admit that I was motivated to write this book because of the time in which we live. We had a new Congress and President to kick off 2009, and unless you are walking around with horse blinders on, you know what is taking place both politically and economically in these United States.

I believe that this book will be appealing to a wide audience of readers, particularly those who may not consider themselves conservative. Perhaps the appeal will be of minimal significance to scholars, intellectuals, and so-called experts. But perhaps this book may be the impetus for some of you to be more involved, to hold our elected officials accountable for what they do or fail to do, or to appreciate the objective reporting of the news when it actually takes place. In any case, it is my hope that you will be enlightened, informed, and somewhat entertained. And,

I might add, that it is perfectly acceptable to laugh a little, yell out loud, or maybe just pump a fist in the air every now and then. I hope that our pondering will lead us to take action in defending the principles that have made America great.

In the King James Version of the New Testament, Matthew chapter 13, there is an interesting parable that likens the kingdom of heaven to a man who sowed good seed in his field. After planting the wheat, his enemy came and sowed tares among the wheat. When the servants came to him afterward, they inquired about the good seed, and why there were now tares sown amongst the wheat; to which the owner of the field replied: "An enemy hath done this." The parable goes on to conclude that the only way to do away with the tares without destroying the crop is to wait until the time of the harvest, and then gather the tares from among the mature crop, bundle, and then burn them. Speaking in a politically figurative sense only, the time of the harvest is now to weed out corrupt politicians.

Finally, I make no apologies for the fact that I have written this book from a conservative viewpoint. It is my belief that if individuals take the time to honestly and objectively digest conservatism, they will come to the conclusion that it makes good sense when compared with other political alternatives. It is also my belief that just because there may not be enough strong conservative voices in our current government, that it does not mean conservatism is irrelevant. I will admit, however, that there are not enough elected conservative voices that are either willing or able to carry the conservative message to a nation that is starving for it, whether they know it or not. That does not mean, however, that I believe that all republicans walk on water, or that all democrats are slime. I believe in limited local and national government, low taxes for all who pay them, sensible regulation, strong national defense, and that every human being matters, to name just a few.

I cannot say enough to thank those who have had a hand in this project. I thank my parents, Darrell and Sarah Reed, for bringing me into this world and teaching me right from wrong; and for my in-laws, John and Betty Wyeth, for raising a God-fearing family. I thank both my father and father-in-law for their service to our country, heroes for their willingness to do so. I thank my siblings, Cindy (Reed) Shrack, Richard Reed, and Ron Reed for their support; though I am sure my brothers were unaware that I had even read a whole lot of books, let alone actually having now written one! I thank each of my children, Karali (Reed) Brackney, Kaela (Reed) Athay, Nathanial Reed, and Krista Reed, as well as the spouses of my married children, Trevor and Mike; each of whom have been very supportive of my efforts. I also thank those in my extended family for all the words of encouragement and support. I want to also give a special thank you to Rick and Kim Nitta and Annette Rothman for their insight and support. All of you and those friends I have not mentioned will probably never completely grasp the level of appreciation and profound respect I have for each of you for your positive encouragement and influence. And finally, to God I give the glory and honor that is rightfully His for all my success as well as the continuous effort to appreciate more fully the adversity experienced along the way. Please enjoy.

BY THE PEOPLE, FOR THE PEOPLE

"We hold these truths to be self-evident, that all men are created equal, that they are endowed by their Creator with certain
inalienable rights; that among these are life, liberty, and the
pursuit of happiness. That to secure these rights, governments
are instituted among men, deriving their just powers from the
consent of the governed ... "[1] It seems to me that practically
anyone, with very little guidance or motivation, is capable of
not only comprehending these words, but actually gaining a
sound understanding of the meaning of this well-known phrase
from the Declaration of Independence. I wonder how much
better America would be if more of us adopted these words as
our own, as if spoken in the first person. Instead, many seem to
have accepted, quite readily, the attitude that our involvement
in politics is best observed from the sidelines where we do not
have to be concerned about the messy details. I am painfully
aware that we live in an era of "spoon feeding," when, even with
the right motivation, many people still seem to choose to be
uninformed or remain apathetic relative to the significance of
our founding documents.

Those who govern in our system do so by the consent of
the governed and we must never be content to only observe
from the sidelines as matters of utmost significance regarding
our liberties being diminished. How often have we all heard
the phrase "it's just politics"? We often hear it from the media
and those who cover politics, as well as from the office holders themselves! The rest of America cannot afford to latch on

to such apathy while elected leaders take us down a road of no return. We must cultivate within ourselves a more profound appreciation of what it means to be an American by being true to the principles of freedom that we commemorate on July 4th.

As a matter of principle, every American, indeed every person who has migrated to this country, that has the capacity, must discover the significance of what it means to be an American with the Declaration of Independence as a foundation. What would follow is a greater desire to understand the Constitution and then to uphold those who will do their utmost to preserve and protect our rights at all costs. By voting for people who are committed to the principles of a representative republic, "we the people" stand a better chance at prosperity in every aspect of our lives. The obvious question is, if the average person is able to develop an appreciation and respect for such history-changing declarations from our founding fathers—then why not, presumably, above average intelligence persons at the highest levels of, "governments … instituted among men?"

We need to take a look at the use of the word "secure" as used within the context of the Declaration of Independence. In order for our rights to be secured, "governments are instituted among men, deriving their just powers from the consent of the governed … "[2] Indeed, in order to secure the rights of life, liberty, and happiness, ordinary people grant their equally ordinary fellow citizens the privilege and responsibility of acting in such a way that is representative of all to whom they are so privileged to represent. Further, it seems appropriate that one who is blessed to receive the honor of representation must understand the expectation to act with the greatest consideration regarding fellow citizens, since they are elevated to a position of determining various aspects about our most basic objective—"life, liberty, and the pursuit of happiness."

The nature of representative government grants power to a limited number of our peers, who then are supposed to act with the utmost responsibility based solely upon ennobling consent from "we the people." I do not hesitate to use the word ennobling; I believe it is accurate. In other words, no one who holds public office in the United States, by means of an authorized election, has power inherent in themselves, only what the people consent to bestow upon them. Thus, we entrust a select few at any given time to bear the burden of responsibility to ever be mindful of the opportunity to safeguard our ability to pursue life, liberty, and happiness. Our pursuit of these ideals must not be compromised by anyone so privileged to represent the people. If it becomes evident, however, that one has occupied an office without fulfilling their obligation to us; then by the voice of the people, the right to govern should be conferred upon another in the attempt to fulfill a duty, bound by oath and built upon the foundation that instructs that they (derive) "their just powers from the consent of the governed."[3]

Every election cycle we witness a seemingly never-ending stream of willing participants, ready to make promises that they are often woefully unprepared to keep, let alone make. And sadly, we eventually witness the pitiful outcome of mere lip service to promises that should have had no business being made in the first place. And often when many of these, our fellow citizens, get elected they develop the mistaken attitude that they have somehow inherited bequeathed powers, which has granted them the power to act as they please without any regard to the people. Foolishness!

The Declaration of Independence states "that whenever any form of government becomes destructive of these ends, it is the right of the people to alter or abolish it ... "[4] The form of government we are talking about is that which has been instituted and completely supports our "pursuit of happiness."[5] I refer to our government as a representative republic; regardless, it is designed to function no matter what we choose to call it because it allows all, who are blessed to live under it, prosperity without fear of retribution from the government, a.k.a. fellow citizens.

There was a time in our history that compelled the people to overthrow tyrannical governments in order to progress as a free and independent nation. However, the founding fathers stated in the Declaration of Independence that established government should not be "changed for light and transient causes." We should never consider freedom as *light* or *transient*. I am humbled to be an American; but at the same time, I am also proud to be an American! No citizen of this country should be made to feel ashamed for expressing patriotism, nor should patriotism ever be politicized, since being patriotic knows no party. Since there are various ways of expressing patriotism, differences should not be perceived as an automatic dismissal of a conflicting political viewpoint, we cannot afford to play "politics" with something that is protected by the Constitution.

There is so much that is right with America today. Granted, I make such a statement in light of the fact that we have witnessed some very serious economic turmoil at home over the last few years, as well as unrest over a terror war rooted in extreme hatred under the guise of religion. The collapse of Fannie Mae and Freddie Mac, the AIG bailout, the overall deterioration of financial markets, investment bank problems, and bank failures, the housing market downfall due to the subprime market, the troublesome U.S. automobile industry mingled with government tampering, and the overall lack of consumer confidence in the economy; not to mention the health care "crisis," have combined to create a recipe for uncertain times. It is a recipe tailor made for some to believe that they have a right to make it better by expanding government over the will of the people. And the signing of the largest spending bill in the history of mankind by President Obama, on the heels of a huge bailout bill signed by President Bush, translates into the incapacity to assess the impact of such turbulent times for many years to come, irrespective of what we have been, or will be told by either administration. There is an obvious lack of accountability and transparency among political operatives today, even though we have been told that things like transparency and accountability would be an essential part of the equation by many a candidate.

Naturally, one can choose to focus on the negative aspects and lament about all that is seemingly wrong with America; that takes very little effort. However, it does require a knack for pessimism. There are those who seem to be always living under the belief that things are never good enough: too many poor; too many uninsured; too many unemployed; too many this, too many that. And God be with anyone who believes that personal responsibility is still an important aspect of being a citizen in this country. Bad things happen for which there is sometimes no explanation. But that does not mean that those in government are supposed to step in and try to make things better because they know what is in the best interest of "we the people."

I believe that many of my fellow citizens are as optimistic as I and will never give up on the things we believe are necessary to keep America great, even though many in politics fight against such optimism because of the power they so desperately crave, and which power they recognize will be taken away if their constituents adopt more of a can-do outlook on life. Many politicians, the current administration included, love using fear tactics to persuade the ignorant in our society to follow them; they are aware of the apathy among many of our citizens and that most people just do not take the time to be informed. For instance, Mr. Obama and Mr. Biden can talk all they want about how the "stimulus" money has turned the economy around, but it does not change reality. First of all, it is next to impossible for anyone in government to account for that kind of money, and secondly, what takes place any other time when our nation experiences economic downturns or serious setbacks? That's right; it typically rebounds, and will do so much quicker if government stays out of it. A lot of bureaucrats in Washington cannot seem to grasp the idea of the ebb and flow of our diverse and complex economic system.

As a people, we need to focus on the public servants who are not only *not* measuring up, but who, indeed, may be doing irreparable damage that will adversely effect generations to come, unless there is a course alteration. Every few years, we get to re-evaluate the employment status of those elected to represent us. Of course, there is excessive greed that will probably never be taken from our system, whether politically or economically, but that does not mean that we should abandon the greatest capitalistic endeavor ever known in the history of the world. Do people honestly believe that the government can do those things that are better left to the private sector such as entrepreneurialism, job creation, wealth creation, and the overall motivation of individuals to go out and make the continuous effort to be as successful as possible?

Naturally, there is failure and risk that are associated with any endeavor in a capitalistic system. However, it should not be left to the government to make decisions when it comes to righting what they perceive as being the wrongs that are experienced by those who try and may occasionally experience failure. It is funny, in a sick sort of way, how many politicians completely embrace their own love affair with irresponsibility and a lack of accountability and then seek comfort and support from those they believe to be suffering needlessly among us. Government cannot force me to be generous. Everyone must square their personal philosophy when it comes to helping their fellow man, and then be prepared to account for those actions someday. Rest assured that such an accounting will be to a much higher power than government. The foundation for this book rests upon my commitment to see the topic of accountability and adherence to constitutional principles by our elected leaders, completely and totally observed; and that we, as a people, might insist that such things not remain an obscurity in Washington, D.C.

If there are portions of this book that seem overly critical or negative of some of our most prominent citizens, remember I am using the exact words spoken by these same people, and then offering my personal observations. The most justifiable condemnation is often that of our own doing.

Many people in elected public service often have no problem, whether intentionally or not, making themselves look foolish—all it usually takes is for the mouth to be open and words to come out. Accountability seems to be a forgotten principle by some who serve us. Since the servant label is the way that many in office often characterize themselves, it seems to me that such a servant ought to commit himself to being at least a dutiful servant, and at best, a willing servant who is steadfastly devoted to the utmost integrity and dignity since they serve "we the people." We have a long way to go to get our elected officials to fully grasp the idea that serving the people is what they are elected to do, not rule with unmitigated power.

Those elected to represent us must be willing to do so in every way without expectation of anything in return. What they can and should expect, however, is to collect a taxpayer funded paycheck and perhaps renewed success at the ballot box. Most people who occupy an elected position in our country sought such a position on their own, without coercion. Scrutiny of our public officials is often times brutal, and I would imagine even more so from their perspective. Moreover, we do not owe any elected politician the least form of allegiance; no one has a right to an elected office, or an appointed office for that matter. So often we see those elected to office treat with disdain and contempt all those who may disagree with or question their motives.

On the contrary, it is the elected politicians who owe us their allegiance to established constitutional principles that all law abiding citizens seek to uphold. Politicians are supposed to be working for us and if they are doing what they're supposed to be doing, they have no need to worry. Often politicians are too busy back peddling, attempting to teach us new meanings to words like "stupidly," and then celebrating such self-indulgent irresponsibility in the form of a "beer summit," which seems to be nothing more than satisfying an enormous ego, as well as a great photo-op.

When any one of us collects a paycheck from our employer, we can expect that our employer will continue to have specific expectations of labor in exchange for such funds; but if or when our employer believes that we are not fulfilling our end of the agreement(s) for employment we should not be surprised to see a slip of paper with a pink hue. Most employees are held to account for not only what they do, but also what they say. Should we expect anything less from our elected "employees?" Why should the president or any other elected official be afforded so many chances when the rest of us are not normally given the same kinds of opportunities? I would like to know of a single private sector employee in America that is able to grant themselves a pay raise without the approval of their employer regardless of job performance. For many years prior and through 2009 Congress was able to continue garnering some fairly steady pay increases with fairly minimal contesting by the American people. Why do our elected representatives in Washington, D.C., have the power to grant themselves pay raises? Obviously, most of us would support a suspension of such increases in pay when someone is not measuring up. Unfortunately, that is usually a decision we do not get to make.

I want to point out some of the challenges that we, as a nation, face, because of those whose ambition is power and control, whether in politics, business, or the media. The truth cannot be compromised. Of course, there are a lot of politicians who think that the truth is a nuisance, since many of them believe that inconvenient facts simply get in the way of their power grab. I believe my responsibility is to shine a light on the people who, whether intentionally or unintentionally, are making America worse for us and future generations.

I would like to go back to a portion of the Declaration of Independence which seems to be descriptive of the times in which we now live. All Americans who love freedom can appreciate the fact that we are the beneficiaries of the right to pursue happiness. However, when government "becomes destructive of these ends,"[6] there is a mechanism in place that allows the people to take action; it is known as the ability to "institute new government."[7] What is new government? Simply stated, I believe new government translates into new people, but getting new people in government does not always mean better government.

Too often in our society, when government "becomes destructive of these ends," we may become displeased or even angry, but allow our own apathy to get in the way and we might end up complaining to the wrong people. Sometimes we might even complain using rather arbitrary terms instead of actually identifying specific problem areas and then taking action and making needed corrections by lending our voices to the cause. Politicians are not mysterious matter floating around in a place called D.C., though at times it may seem like it. Therefore, we must be able to identify people in government that are being inhibitive or "destructive" of our ability to pursue happiness, among other things, and have the courage to speak out. Once these individuals have been identified, it is up to the people to put them on the path to finding another line of work, preferably in the private sector, in a place where they will have the least impact on the rest of us.

If the people continue electing power-seeking destructionists, I'm not sure what can be done. Uninformed and ignorant people will probably always be at the beck and call of certain politicians who are long on style but short on substance, which can only lead to oppression. Though our institution of "new government" may differ from that of the pioneers of freedom and liberty during our founding; it is nevertheless equally important to the preservation of our way of life.

Most of us would probably agree there are many aspects of our lives that government tends to infringe on; inhibiting our ability to pursue happiness. One example is excessive taxation.

Even though Article 1, Section 8 of the Constitution authorizes congress to levy taxes, it is still somewhat vague. I do not believe that the founding fathers had in mind the kind of tax system that is in place today in America. We are not supposed to have taxation without representation; though I will leave it to responsible citizens to determine how that is working out. We need to get back to the time of our founding when even the lay person could understand political speech. Unfortunately, we have accepted the notion that the most qualified people who can run government, in many cases must come from the ranks of lawyers. I do not believe that this is what the founding fathers had in mind, even though most of them were from the elite educated class of the time.

It is true that people like Alexander Hamilton and James Madison believed that the federal government had the power to levy taxes and that the people should be obligated to pay such taxes; but lawyers and taxes are much different today and conjure up much different images in the minds of people than perhaps they once did a couple centuries ago. Take a look at nearly any bill and you will probably agree that lawyers have managed to demonstrate their pension for ambiguity through their attempt to destroy common sense language. I believe it is an attempt to keep as many people uninformed as possible by persuading them to ignore complex legal speak. Even those responsible for casting a vote on such legislation on our behalf often do not understand what they are voting for—and most of them are lawyers too! We simply trust the word of those who sit in Congress, that they have our best interests at heart when they vote for legislation which they often do not understand, nor have taken the time to read in many instances.

I believe most of us would agree that those who serve in elected government often take more of our money than what should actually be allowed by law. We ought to acknowledge the fact that some who run government today seem overjoyed at the prospect of taking our money, even though they may act

25

as if they are not. They like to pretend that their reasons for doing so help the disadvantaged, when really all it often ends up doing is putting the rest of us on the path to being disadvantaged ourselves through their continuous efforts to take more and more from those who contribute. We must do more to show our displeasure with the government's rape of our hard work and ingenuity. Actually, we cannot afford to engage in passive attempts to discourage Congress from taking our hard earned income, but we must aggressively oppose every attempt by our government to enact, by legislation, the social notion of redistribution in all its heinous forms, no matter how some attempt to dress it up as compassion for those who lack.

For those like Joe Biden, who seek nobility because you believe you could be paying more to the government, or that it is your "patriotic" duty to pay more; be my guest, pay all you want, but please do not expect those of us who believe that the government is already engaging in "legal" theft, to follow suit. Experience has shown that when government takes more than it should from us, that it simply comes up with more ways to spend it. Look at the results of miserable government fiduciary mismanagement over the last seventy-five years or so and you will probably agree. Once the practitioners of excessive taxation and redistribution have been identified, there is only one thing left to do: hold them to account for their "legalized" thievery and vote them out of office. Unfortunately, politicians have been some of the most gluttonous people in the world with our money, and have persuaded many unsuspecting voters into their vortex of redistributing some of the peoples' money in the ways they see fit. Fortunately, we can control more of what we work for by voting for those committed to fiscal responsibility, and at the appropriate time, institute an overhaul by establishing "new government" in favor of those who understand how to keep taxes low and control spending.

FANNIE MAE, FREDDIE MAC AND POLITICIANS AS EXPERTS ON THE ECONOMY

Here is another aspect about some of our elected officials that I cannot imagine any of their mothers being too proud of: accepting campaign contributions from organizations that supposedly exist to assist low income folks, not only get into a home, but be able to remain in that home. I am referring to the implosion of Fannie Mae and Freddie Mac. Fannie and Freddie "control half [of] the $12 trillion U.S. housing market ... "[8] Many politicians have been guilty of accepting contributions from Fannie Mae and Freddie Mac.[9] At the top of the list posted on September 18, 2008: Chris Dodd, Barack Obama, and John Kerry. Ironically, the top three happen to be democrats, and to be fair, many names appear on the list of politicians who have accepted money in varying amounts, like republicans John McCain and Bob Bennett. If there are questionable financial practices going on in politics, then the people have a right to know about it, no matter how seemingly insignificant. Regardless of what McCain/Feingold purported, and regardless of the Supreme Court's decision allowing corporations to make financial contributions to candidates, money from special interests whose intentions are corrupt will always find its way to corruptible politicians.

On Tuesday, September 23, 2008, Senator Chris Dodd, made these comments in his opening remarks at a hearing on Capitol

Hill to members of the Bush administration and the Chairman of the Federal Reserve, Ben Bernanke: "It is clear that our current economic circumstances demand that we rethink, reform, and modernize supervision of the financial services industry. Certain basic principles should form the foundation for reform. We need a leader in the White House who will ensure that regulators are strong cops on the beat and do not turn a blind eye to reckless lending practices ... We need to ensure that all institutions that pose a risk to our financial system and taxpayers are carefully and sensibly supervised."[10]

Chris Dodd's statement is a perfect example of politicians looking stupid by opening their mouths. In the first place, at the time Mr. Dodd made this statement, he was no less than the Senate Banking Committee Chairman, of the party in the majority since 2006! In the opening paragraph of his prepared statement, the senator said that, "I can only conclude that it is not just our economy that is at risk ... but our constitution, as well."[11] How on earth could he preach such language and keep a straight face? I believe this is referred to as style over substance. I mean no disrespect to the senator, but it would have seemed more appropriate for Mr. Dodd to have included in his opening statement, words such as: *I can only conclude that it is not just our economy that is at risk ... but my chairmanship position on this committee, indeed my job as a United States Senator, because of my lack of attention to detail.* Correct me if I'm wrong, but I always understood that it is the legislature who determines the appropriation of tax dollars under the Constitution. It seems to me like Senator Dodd should have been one of the people responsible for finding regulators who could have served as his "strong cops on the beat" to make sure that sound lending practices were adhered to if he was really that concerned about it.

Fortunately for the people of Connecticut Mr. Dodd has made the dignified decision to not seek reelection by retiring as opposed to submitting himself to another campaign. Perhaps he could see the writing on the wall. In any case I believe it was a good decision.

How many times does the Congress need to reform, modernize, or rethink basic principles that should serve as the foundation for all congressional scrutiny, be it private or political? Where is the oversight for Congress and their hypocrisy? Well, in the case of Mr. Dodd, and every other politician, it is "we the people." And if we are to form a more perfect union, we cannot allow complacency, either by the people or from those who win elections to be the predominant characteristic that governs attitude. Too often, many members of Congress fail to do the things necessary to avert some kind of crisis, and then afterward feign disgust about the consequences to make it look as if they really care. Members of Congress must be held to account for playing games with the American people and then thinking that they can ride up on a great stallion to save the day. We must be vigilant when it comes to holding our elected officials to account for their actions; if we fail to, we have no room to complain.

To understand the incredibly irresponsive actions of government as it relates to Fannie Mae and Freddie Mac, we must understand some of the events leading up to the housing crises. President George H. W. Bush signed into law H.R. 5334, which was supposed to help protect the people. On that occasion, the president said: "This bill establishes a sound regulatory structure for Government-sponsored enterprises (GSEs)..."[12] He also stated that "it establishes a means to protect taxpayers from the possible risks posed by GSEs in housing finance. This bill creates a regulator within the Department of Housing and Urban Development (HUD) to ensure that the housing GSEs are adequately capitalized and operated safely."[13] Housing GSEs like Fannie Mae and Freddie Mac, for instance.

It seems that President George H. W. Bush would have accommodated Mr. Dodd many years ago by establishing his precious "cops on the beat." However, like many bills that become law in this country, the Housing and Community Development Act of 1992 was nothing more than a token gesture to make some politicians and a few of the people feel good about themselves while accomplishing very little.

We have to wonder what it is that Dodd or anyone else in Congress has done all these years to ensure that those accountable for enforcing strict regulation of GSEs like Fannie and Freddie did their jobs. Do Dodd or other lawmakers who participated in crafting legislation that became law not understand the law that it created? I will be the first to admit that I am not in favor of strengthening an already fully functioning, often out-of-control bureaucracy, regardless of how well-intentioned; but in the case of George H. W. Bush signing a bill designed to regulate GSEs—it would seem that Dodd got what he wanted. Yet, what was done to enforce regulation of GSEs like Fannie and Freddie? Not a lot, in fact; the two mortgage giants were given special privileges because of their government charter, especially as it relates to Mortgage Backed Securities and Security and Exchange Commission (SEC) regulations. But in Congress, instead of worrying about things that have much more important consequences, like the impact of a potential housing crash, it seems like our esteemed leaders would rather convene congressional hearings to scrutinize and grill members of a president's cabinet, pro baseball players about steroid use, or CEO's and the mode of travel they choose to employ, or whatever they determine is fit for their outrage. So whenever the Congress is concerned or suspicious of the actions of anyone, or they believe something is not being regulated to their satisfaction; they simply call a hearing because that is what they seem to do best; hold other people to account.

The Administration of President George W. Bush actually proposed the creation of a new agency to try and reign in the downward spiral of Fannie Mae and Freddie Mac. Unfortunately for taxpayers, his bid was unsuccessful. It is interesting to note, however, some of the details not only of the proposal, but what some in Congress actually thought about it. Stephen Labaton writes that, "Under the plan, disclosed at a Congressional hearing today, a new agency would be created within the Treasury Department to assume supervision of Fannie Mae and Freddie Mac, the government-sponsored companies that are the two largest players in the mortgage lending industry."[14] I am not sure what the difference would have been to essentially transfer the responsibility to regulate Fannie and Freddie from HUD to Treasury. And to be fair, both democrats and republicans are to blame. However, democrats seem to make the most noise when it comes to such issues as oversight and regulation. Regardless, it seems to me that it would have made more sense to enforce the laws that had already been created regarding regulatory oversight of Fannie and Freddie; but unfortunately in Washington, D.C., it does not always make sense to do the obvious.

It is curious to ponder why the Congress did not pay more attention to this matter, especially since there were plenty members of Congress that had received campaign contributions from Fannie and Freddie over the years; and that ultimately, information like that would eventually make its way to the rest of us. You would think that members of Congress would have been smarter than that; evidently not. Is it possible that the recipients of campaign contributions could have turned the other way in the midst of all the troubles that Fannie and Freddie were experiencing? "At the time, the companies and their allies beat back efforts for tougher oversight by the Treasury Department, the Federal Deposit Insurance Corporation, or the Federal Reserve. Supporters of the companies said efforts to regulate the lenders tightly under those agencies might diminish their ability to finance loans for lower-income families."[15] What an interesting dichotomy, politicians like Dodd deriding the Bush administration for not being aggressive enough to establish greater regulatory control (and even blocking the presidents efforts do so), yet at the same time turning a blind eye to enforcement when it was so desperately needed—incredible!

"Among the groups denouncing the proposal today were the National Association of Home Builders and Congressional Democrats who fear that tighter regulation of the companies could sharply reduce their commitment to financing low-income and affordable housing. 'These two entities—Fannie Mae and Freddie Mac—are not facing any kind of crises,'" said Representative Barney Frank of Massachusetts, the ranking democrat on the Financial Services Committee. "The more people exaggerate these problems, the more pressure there is on these companies, the less we will see in terms of affordable housing."

Representative Melvin L. Watt, democrat of North Carolina, agreed. "I don't see much other than a shell game going on here, moving something from one agency to another and in the process weakening the bargaining power of poorer families and their ability to get affordable housing," Mr. Watt said.[16] Need I remind anyone that all of this took place in 2003, just a few years before you know what hit the fan? Where is the real outrage from the American people toward irresponsible and conniving politicians? Why do we continue to let business as usual rule the day?

What might have happened if people like Mr. Dodd and Mr. Frank had been more focused on doing the right thing for the American people? The financial circumstances the country experienced may have been drastically curtailed, perhaps averted altogether, particularly in the housing sector. We would have most likely experienced some financial setbacks, but I do not believe it would have been as rough as it actually was, or is, depending on your viewpoint. But like a lot of things in Washington, many hands are turned with their palms up, ready to receive as much cash as possible to satisfy an unhealthy greed. I cannot imagine what Mr. Frank's position would have been had he received even more than the $42,000 in campaign contributions from the two failing companies. And not to be outdone, Mr. Watt talking about such significant matters as if it were nothing more than a carnival shell game—unbelievable! It is amazing that such people continue to possess the audacity to pontificate from their high and mighty positions, spewing such nonsense and outright political heresy. Who do these people think they are?

In nearly every election, national or otherwise, we often here rhetoric from both democrats and republicans about how out of touch with America the other party is. I believe it is safe to say that neither party is really in touch with regular folks because of self-imagined elitism when compared to the rest of us. It would be refreshing to have both Houses of Congress, as well as the Executive Branch, actually put aside their enormous egos, to get things done on behalf of the American people like they always *talk* about doing. And for the most part, "we the people" would be happy if they would just keep their noses out of our business; let decent, honest, hard-working people worry about the success of the economy.

The following statement came from Senator Dodd's Website: "The administration's failure to prevent bad lending practices has caused unprecedented hardship in the form of record foreclosures and market turmoil…the administration has refused to develop or support any meaningful effort to help keep Americans in their homes and preserve efficiency and stability in our markets."[17] This is beyond believable, not to mention a completely fabricated statement, and the Senator has to know it. "Prevent bad lending practices?" Dodd knows that the impetus behind these "practices" was his own party putting pressure on financial institutions to make loans available to the financially "down-trodden" in communities where perhaps some people were not quite credit worthy.

First of all, I did not realize that the President of the United States was the Chief Lending Officer, appointed to determine credit worthiness of borrowers! Second, I had no idea that it was the job of the President to prevent borrowers from being subjected to foreclosure. Third, what about the personal responsibility of every American who enters into a loan agreement to buy a house? And fourth, Dodd and many of his counterparts in Congress refused to do anything to avert possible crises. The collapse in the housing industry cannot be entirely placed upon the backs of "predatory lenders," though some shared responsibility exists. How Senator Dodd could show his face in public, after making such unbelievable statements and at the same time believing that he had been doing an effective job for the people of his state, is beyond me. That goes for people like Representatives Watt and Frank as well. It does not help when people like Mr. Dodd seem to be paralyzed with inaction (other than when accusing Bush) and fail to do what is necessary to actually enforce legislation that is designed to protect the people. Even the Scarecrow on *The Wizard of Oz* would have had enough of a brain to recognize the complicity of politicians in the debacle associated with the sub-prime mortgage market and the struggles experienced by many banks and other lending institutions because of it.

Again, we have to acknowledge that predatory lending does take place, probably more often than we would care to admit. But in Washington, D.C., it is often a one way street and it most often only goes in whatever direction that corrupt politicians determine. So it is really not that surprising when we do not hear even one politician admitting that he could be responsible for the downfall of Fannie and Freddie, because he failed to hold the regulators' feet to the fire. Is it possible that there were not enough regulations already in place? I doubt that very seriously. I suspect like most things in Washington, too many who are supposed to be representing us fail to enforce regulation because it might actually mean less power or money for themselves. Perhaps Mr. Dodd was one of the few people actually listening to the Wizard when he nervously quipped: "Pay no attention to the man behind the curtain."

Can anyone believe the kind of mumbo jumbo that Dodd published on his official Web site? Are we to understand that the senator at that time did not have enough experience in the

United States Senate to understand the Constitution's Article 1, Section 8? Mr. Dodd was a member of the Senate in 2003 when President Bush proposed regulatory overhauls of the housing finance industry. Where was Mr. Dodd back then? Did he speak out in support of proposed legislation; author legislation himself; do anything to bring forward his own version of reform? No, it seems to have been easier for him and many others to point the finger of blame at someone else instead of accepting responsibility for his own actions. Surely there are people in Connecticut and Massachusetts capable of doing a better job of representation than Dodd and Frank. It is up to the voters to face the facts and be aware of allowing people like Dodd and Frank to get a pass. Unfortunately, we know that their situations are not unusual and happen with too much frequency.

I can only imagine what the founding fathers would think of some who occupy the halls of congress today. If it were possible, the founders would probably ask something like: *Do you remember who sent you to Washington and gave you the responsibility to represent the will of the people?* I do not yet believe that the will of the people is corrupt like some who reside in Washington, whose job is to responsibly represent us while forgetting about their personal advancement.

Perhaps some of you believe that someone like Senator Dodd is not that bad for the people of this country, in spite of my attempts to use the Senator's own words to prove otherwise. President Bush addressed the nation relative to the incredible turmoil surrounding the economy. Mr. Dodd made a statement directly after, in which he said, "It is regrettable that forty days before an election it has taken the worst economic crisis in our nation since the Great Depression to finally get the attention of the president. Until this point, the cries for help from millions of Americans being forced from their homes and struggling to make ends meet fell on the president's deaf ears. Now, we face challenges that were entirely preventable and avoidable. The administration has put forth a proposal to address the crisis they helped to create ... the Congress is working around the clock to develop a solution that includes more oversight, stronger protections for taxpayers, and measures that will address the root cause of this crises—the collapse of the housing market."[18] The really incredible thing about his statement is that he hits the nail on the head by admitting that the root cause of the crisis is "the collapse of the housing market," yet he manages to lay blame for it all at the feet of the president. Obviously, the senator had forgotten the incredibly bleak economic times of the recession laden Carter years and the leadership of Ronald Reagan that was instrumental in putting the country on solid footing once again.

So many people, including President Obama, have portrayed the economic downturn as the worst economic crises since the Great Depression. Such a characterization is woefully inaccurate and simply not true. I seemed to have missed all the accolades reserved for the Bush administration when our economy began to rebound after the attacks of 9/11. Republicans were trying to do what they could to avoid problems in the housing sector long before Chris Dodd chided Bush, but democrats simply impeded their attempts to forestall a downturn in the housing market, and then turned right around to put the blame on the other party.

Too many politicians enjoy using the "fear card" to hypnotize people who ought to know better. However, when we hear things over and over about how horrible the economy is, and that it is in the worst shape it has been in since the Depression; it becomes difficult for even reasonably intelligent people to resist piling on. I do not necessarily want the Congress to do more than it needs to do; but since they are the body responsible for creating laws they ought to at least believe in enacting sensible laws. When a member of the U.S. Senate complains because he believes a crisis was "preventable and avoidable," yet did nothing to prevent or avoid it but complain that the president had done nothing, indeed, that the president "helped to create," well, that is difficult to accept. Actually, the right thing for politicians to do is to step aside and let economic prosperity work for all those willing to put forth the effort to make it work for themselves and their families.

The congress is entrusted with the power to send legislation to the president; that is why we have a legislative branch in the first place. Are we to believe that the best work our representatives do is that which is produced when they are backed into a corner and under enormous pressure? Two words should answer that question: bailout package. And why the petty, cheap-shot remark by Senator Dodd about how close we were to an election? I guess that is what we have been reduced to; politicizing an economic "crisis" at a time when the senator knew the people would be going to the polls to elect a new president and new members of congress. Why did it take the president to address such a crisis before the Chairman of the Senate Banking Committee finally stood up to take notice? What does that say about the senator's ability to lead? I wonder if the Congress would still be trying to figure out what to do had Bush not been willing to take the lead. Sadly, this is what we had to deal with during the Bush years: whiners and complainers in Congress, but no leadership.

Maybe Congress enjoys putting in overtime on occasion. After all, Senator Dodd did say that the Congress was "working around the clock." I believe a lot of the American people are as fed up as I am with all the "politics" happening inside the Beltway. I admit that I was not always a fan of some of the things that President Bush did while he was in office. The fact that he was not a sound conservative regarding fiscal policy was troubling. And that he felt obligated to start the bailout train rolling down the tracks, having now gained so much more negative momentum, is also distressing. Many conservative politicians spend far too much time trying to be liked by everybody instead of advocating conservative principles that will ultimately benefit everyone, not just a select group.

The problems with Fannie and Freddie, the Investment Banks, AIG, the automotive industry, and a host of other sectors, is the fact that their challenges extended well beyond the president and Congress. However, to be a politician and be unwilling to admit wrongdoing or culpability, and all the while pointing the finger of scorn toward anyone but the person in the mirror is the height of hypocrisy. There seems to be what I would call an absence of dignity equity on the part of many politicians in Washington. Even though the guilty parties know who they are in Congress, they always seem to try and plead their innocence to any sympathetic listening ear and the truth seldom comes out.

One of the seemingly more difficult challenges that continue to plague the American people is the inability of Congress to legislate responsibly. It is true that no amount of legislation can compensate for a lack of ethical behavior among the private sector; nor in the halls of Congress. However, Congress can and must police their own efforts before they can point the finger of scorn at anyone in the private sector. How dare members of Congress attach all the special interest, pork barrel spending waste onto any piece of meaningful legislation! And how dare Mr. Obama tell the American people that the stimulus he signed into law a month into his presidency had no pork or wasteful spending attached to it. That is just not true.

The really scary part about Congress policing itself is that "we the people" are supposed to be the court of last resort; but if enough people disregard the actions of those elected to represent us, regardless of the branch, then I suppose we can conclude in every instance that we get what we deserve. Whether politicians like it or not, they must be responsible to the people, and should be subject to the same consequences as anyone in the private sector. In a perfect world, we would have no need to monitor the conduct of the president, Congress, CEO's or employees. In such a world, we would not be in a state of wonder about the present plight of our economy and the outcome of billions of taxpayer dollars in a bailout package.

The tenants of the *Golden Rule* seem to have been forgotten because there is too much greed, selfishness, and abuse of power that tends to govern the actions of some who walk among us. And as a result, over the last couple of decades, a lot of unsuspecting, hard-working Americans have lost confidence that the system will do the right thing for the people. Corporate America, Wall Street, and private investors may never lose their lust for greed when it comes to cash, even at the expense of the average Joe; some people just do not care about others; look at Bernie Madoff. But by the same token, politicians need to act responsibly and control their greed for power and control.

Undoubtedly, there is too much partisanship in the halls of Congress. Unfortunately, the American people bare the brunt of such divisiveness in Washington. So much has been made of the historic bailout of parts of Wall Street and certain sectors in Corporate America. It will be years before we will know how effective the bailout money will have been; I doubt that anything as humungous as the billions of dollars allocated to "rescue" our economy will ever be properly accounted for, no matter how supporters of the bailout package articulate its effectiveness. However, there are some things that we do know, such as Nancy Pelosi making this statement "…when was the last time someone asked you for $700 billion? It is a number that is staggering, but tells us only the costs of the Bush administration's failed economic policies—policies built on budgetary recklessness, on an anything goes mentality, with no regulation, no supervision, and no discipline in the system. Democrats believe in the free market, which can and does create jobs, wealth, and capital, but left to its own devices it has created chaos."[19] Such a statement seems to be destructive and counterproductive partisanship; not to mention the biggest pile of slop imaginable! Yet, where is anyone in the mainstream media that has called the Speaker out for such reckless comments. Her language is typical of one who seems to have no regard for how the economy works in our capitalistic system. If she or any of her cronies really understood, they would have wasted little time in cutting taxes for everyone who pays them. Pelosi cannot possibly expect that any of us believes that she actually supports the "free market, which can and does create jobs, wealth, and capital ... " because in reality, she has displayed behavior that is quite different than her professed belief in the free market.

I believe that the people would like to see less blaming and complaining from our elected leaders and more cooperation. This undeserved rebuke by the Speaker is evidence of the true nature and partisanship of many like Nancy Pelosi who are not as concerned about bipartisanship, but rather having things done their way. It is up to us to remind these people that they serve at the discretion of the American people and no one else.

When the Speaker of the House makes such outrageous claims, seemingly based on raw emotion, not reason; it is truly amazing to behold. It does seem to be quite a stretch for her to suggest that everyone is against free markets, job creation, wealth, and capital except for democrats. If democrats are so concerned about wealth creation, free markets, and capital preservation, then why not do something really meaningful, like lower the marginal tax rates for businesses? Why not lower capital gains taxes, or even eliminate them for a while to see what kind of boost that would have on the economy? End the burdensome regulations and tax laws that have chased companies from within our borders and forced many of them to set up shop out of the country, which may never be reversed due to the fact that businesses have adjusted to the cheap cost of producing goods in Asia, Mexico, and elsewhere; even though it means fewer jobs for Americans. Again, we have a very prominent politician pointing the finger of blame at someone else instead of being a true leader for the people.

Everyone knows that it is corporations, big and small businesses, and a host of other people in America that actually create the jobs for the vast majority of citizens. Politicians in Washington should make it easier for the job creators to hire the masses that actually make up the middle class. I have never known an unemployed person, or a politician, who created a private sector job. Personally, I want economic stability and friendly tax policy for everyone so that I can be confident about maintaining gainful employment, knowing that a company is not headed overseas because of unfriendly tax policy here. What most people want is for Washington to step out of the way and let the American entrepreneurial spirit flourish. What we do not need or want is for Washington to get involved in something that is better left to the private sector; or pretend that what they are doing is actually going to benefit anyone. The prospects are potentially scary and we had better wake up to what is being done before our very eyes, seemingly all in the name of power and control.

Millions of Americans (and even those here illegally) are the beneficiaries of the greatest governmental and political system ever devised by man. We cannot forget that this country was established by a people escaping tyranny through monarchial control, a people longing to be free. It seems to be that some politicians today want to take away from us our freedom and liberty. Do we need regulation and oversight in government and business today? Yes, because man has a pension for corruptness. However, the foundations of our system of government and economic prosperity are sound, even if McCain failed to vigorously defend that position during the presidential campaign of 2008. And it is ironic how Obama, as president even admitted to the soundness of our economy when he said: "You should also know that the money you've deposited in banks across the country is safe; your insurance is secure; and you can rely on the continued operation of our financial system."[20] It sounds a whole lot like Mr. Obama believed that the fundamentals of our economy were sound just a few months after McCain had made a similar statement and was hammered for it. Why all the false pretense and hand wringing over McCain's statement? American's who have any sense know that the economic fundamentals of our country were just as sound in the midst of the presidential campaign as they are now. I do not want our economic system to be tainted by the hand of government, even to the extent that it now is. It is not right that as of this moment, the government is saddling my children and unborn grandchildren with a load of debt undeserving of any generation.

Politicians ought to lead the way, since they are so visible, by showing the rest of America how to communicate and get things done even though agreement is often difficult to come by. Such effort will require honesty, beginning with the Commander in Chief. We tend to elevate prominent people in our society, for right or wrong, as role models for our young people. I submit that it is time for all politicians to begin today to set the right kind of example that we would all be willing to emulate. The first order of business is to weed out corrupt politicians and replace them with those who respect "government of the people, by the people, for the people," and who are not above being accountable to the people. We need politicians who are as courageous as Abraham Lincoln, not just to give a great speech like he did at Gettysburg, but who will be honest and forthright, willing to act with conviction on those principles that will continue to preserve us as a nation.

POLITICAL DISCOURSE

According to the United States Constitution, there are relatively few requirements necessary to be a member of either House; namely, "No person shall be a Representative who shall not have attained to the age of twenty-five years, and been seven years a citizen of the United States, and who shall not, when elected, be an inhabitant of that state in which he shall be chosen."[21] To become a member of the Senate, "No person shall be a Senator who shall not have attained to the age of thirty years, and been nine years a citizen of the United States, and who shall not, when elected, be an inhabitant of that State for which he shall be chosen."[22] Basically, you need to be a resident of the state you want to represent, meet the requirement as a citizen of the

United States, and have attained the required age. To become president, "No person except a natural born citizen ... shall be eligible to the Office of President; neither shall any person be eligible to that office who shall not have attained to the age of thirty-five years, and been fourteen years a resident within the United States."[23] Alright, big deal!

Well, for starters we're not accustomed to the kind of language that was used back in the eighteenth century when the Constitution was drafted. Notwithstanding, those who appreciate the Constitution realize that there are minimal qualifications required in order to be qualified to serve in either the Legislative or Executive Branches of the government. This does not necessarily mean that just because you have a pulse and you meet the minimum standards prescribed, that serving in elected office is your ultimate destiny. As a nation, we need to be reasonably assured that those we elect have the determination to serve "we the people."

Experience alone should not be the determining factor in choosing our elected officials. All too often, people with more experience has come to mean the person who has perfected the craft of language. What I mean by that is that there are those who have developed the ability to speak well in front of people. The more practice one has in speaking to a crowd or in front of the camera, the better one tends to become in the art of language that is often deceiving. And if a few random facts are mingled in with a good delivery, that usually is enough to pacify listeners. The better one becomes in the art of language as a craft, the more equipped one becomes in the ability to make people believe what they want them to believe. We probably all remember this one: "I did not have sex with that woman, Ms. Lewinsky." Please do not jump to any conclusions. Not everyone who has the ability to speak well in public is deliberately setting out to deceive; but it does require that we make the effort to use good judgment when making decisions about who will represent us because character does matter.

Perhaps the reason so many unprincipled lawyers get into politics is because they know that they can manipulate most in the general public. I actually have nothing against lawyers; it is probably nice to retain the services of one should circumstances require it. I suppose what I am trying to say is that sometimes I have a problem with the lawyer's craft; but like any other profession, it's usually a few slime balls that force everyone else to work twice as hard to obtain, and then maintain, credibility. Since I have not attended law school, I can only presume that law school students receive training regarding how to best persuade listeners to a particular point-of-view, a viewpoint that may not always have the truth as its foundation. We should not be surprised what has become of the nature of politics today given the abundance of lawyers in Congress, as well as the Oval Office. However, not all politicians are out to trick and deceive people regardless of their previous professional background. Perhaps the most profound principle regarding the personal core beliefs and convictions of a politician is to note their actions, as opposed to what their tongues may deliver.

Most Christians are familiar with the well-known phrase: "Wherefore by their fruits ye shall know them."[24] In other words, good seed will yield quality fruit, not a weed or a thistle. For me it is also analogous to those occasions when I was out too late as a teenager with my brothers; and while on the way home, trying to come up with a story to explain to our father the reason for our lateness. Naturally, my brothers and I always hoped that the final version of our "story" sounded plausible; a scary proposition then, and nearly gives me the shivers thinking about it now. Typically, most parents have the uncanny ability to recognize a ration of lies when they hear it; just like most of the American people happen to be pretty good about recognizing the same sort of lies flowing from the mouth of a rotten politician. The ultimate question is this: Do the American people really care anymore? It seems to me that if enough of the people really like a member of Congress, there is no end to how many elections he or she can win, since term limits are not a factor. In today's world of politics, it does not seem to matter what past misdeeds may have been committed, not to mention indiscretions that may have been committed during time in office; electability often has very little or nothing at all to do with integrity and decency. Why? We often elect people based upon much lesser qualities; like the superficiality of one's looks or the way a candidate speaks. Personality and likeability are probably important, but should not be the determining factor when it comes time to cast our vote. Integrity still matters!

I believe those who run for public office should be motivated by statements such as the following: "And for the support of this Declaration, with a firm reliance on the protection of Divine Providence, we mutually pledge to each other our lives, our fortunes, and our sacred honor."[25] I would like to believe that there are still those serving among us today that actually aspire to such high ideals. Imagine if those who served us today adopted the attitude that nothing was more important, or worth more, than their lives, fortunes, and sacred honor. I'm willing to bet that we would eliminate most things that are considered to be a "crisis" in America; like the obsession for health care reform, if those responsible for making laws in this country were willing to "pledge" their very lives in exchange for superfluous and mandated legislation. In many ways, it would be extremely pleasing to hear the kind of language that was used at the time of our nation's founding. It just seems that it might foster a greater desire within each of us to use more civility and respect. Profane language is so common today that we seem to have accepted it as normal instead of being repulsed by it. At times of disagreement or conflict, we cannot afford to tarnish civil discord by saying something later or demonstrating by our conduct, a complete lack of courtesy.

The unfortunate and sad truth about seeking public office today is that elites have corrupted the laws regulating seeking political office so that it has become difficult for an "outsider" to defeat an incumbent; though it does happen. I do not believe the founding fathers could have envisioned the system they created evolving to give an unfair advantage to incumbents. When a majority of incumbents continue to win election after election, laws are created to give strength to such incumbents and make it more difficult for challengers in the future, not to mention the legalese which the average person has difficulty understanding, let alone reading. During the 2008 presidential campaign, then Senator Obama touted his campaign of "change," which we have since learned he could not have meant the kind of change that we would actually support. When politicians try to please everyone, usually they end up putting themselves between the proverbial "rock and a hard place."

Maybe there is a code or pact that members of Congress and the president enter into when they take office. I understand that they all take an oath of office affirming that they will uphold and defend the Constitution. The oath of office doesn't seem to be adequate for a lot of elected officials because many do not seem to be defending the Constitution, notwithstanding the phrase, "So help me God," usually included at the end of all oaths of office. Something else that I really do not understand is the partisan animosity that is so pervasive among many in our system of government today. I may make comments you do not agree with, or include statements of a politician that you would rather like to forget about, all of which is perfectly fine, but that does not equate to the level of animosity and hate. Too many people in our society during recent times have been demonized because they have expressed an opposing viewpoint. The right to dissent without fear is uniquely American. It is wrong that practically every person who runs for public office has their own agenda, and it often does not coincide with that of the people. Most of us simply want politicians to be there for us should we need them to step in to listen to our grievances, and then act with haste to redress such concerns.

Mr. Obama talked during the campaign about how he was going to lead the bipartisan charge in Washington if he were elected; he was going to include the opposition party in a new revolution of bipartisanship, leading the way to building a strong, and I might add, transparent government. Ah, yes, coalition building at its best! I contend that he seems to have forgotten about his pledge because his administration wasted no time trying to ramrod the so-called stimulus package down the throats of Congress (we the people) during his first month in office; and lo and behold if he did not sign that largely unread piece of legislation and make it the law of the land. I missed the *bipartisan* and *transparent* part.

It seems to be typical of the business-as-usual philosophy that was supposed to have been done away with when Obama got to town. I guess it was just typical campaign rhetoric, the kind of poison I refer to as "politics." Most of us were under the impression that Obama was going to usher in a new era of less talk and more action. Not even a historic victory by Obama seems to have been capable of ushering in a new political era.

TERROR ATTACK, WAR AND RESPONSIBILITY

Shortly after the September 11, 2001, terrorist attacks on the United States, the people of this country came together and united against an evil and intolerant enemy that we have since learned is determined to eliminate our way of life. From politicians to your average Joe, there really seemed to be greater unity among the people; and I believe it was sincere. When more of the facts began to emerge, it was determined, and rightfully so, that Afghanistan became the initial central focus on the so-called "War on Terror;" though the Obama administration seems more concerned about semantics regarding the war for fear they might end up offending the terrorists. For purposes relative to this book, and spelling it out in unmistakable terms for the next generation, I maintain that terrorists' organizations and all who belong to them or support them are nothing less than wickedness and evil masquerading as people . Anyone who believes that he is doing God a favor by the unprovoked slaughtering of other human beings has been ruthlessly deceived. We often hear this phrase repeated by someone characterizing another person's contrition; that they have had a come-to-Jesus moment. The barbaric killers who seem to put themselves on God's side as a means of justifying their homicidal tendencies have no doubt experienced what I like to call a "come-to-Satan moment." Unfortunately for these people, there will be no throng of virgins waiting for them on the other side, as they erroneously surmise.

Ultimately, the focus of the War on Terror shifted to Iraq. This shift in focus was the beginning of the end of our short-lived unification against a common enemy. I suppose that the reasoning in the shift in focus from Afghanistan to Iraq will be argued until hell freezes over. The primary reason the Bush administration gave for going into Iraq was its possession of weapons of mass destruction (WMD). The question was not necessarily whether Iraq actually possessed WMDs; but rather, the location and quantity of such weapons. Everyone knew at that time that Saddam Hussein did possess WMDs, and had even used them on his own people. In light of the fact that WMDs were never located, however, does not dismiss the fact that Hussein did possess them. Indeed, it is important to recognize that there remained justification to go into Iraq.

In the years leading up to September 11, 2001, Saddam Hussein had repeatedly turned his back on the U.S. and the United Nations Security Council (UNSC); his belligerence and defiance regarding a host of UNSC Resolutions became problematic. Unfortunately, for the UN, and ultimately the U.S., the longer Hussein defied these resolutions, the more brazen he became. Admittedly, the Clinton and Bush administrations could have done a better job focusing on Iraq's defiance of the American people. The media focused on the lack of WMDs during the Bush years and worked it like a deep blue feeding frenzy; seemingly forgetting, as a matter of convenience, all the other facts that had been compiled in the case against Saddam. We cannot forget, too, that Saddam had begun subsidizing Palestinian family members of homicide bombers with cash payments.

These and other facts supported the case against Saddam Hussein, irrespective of the lack of WMDs. For those who believe that the United States made a supposed rush to judgment, remember the fact that for many years Iraq made a mockery of the civilized world and the United Nations Security

Council. Thankfully, we had a US Congress that took decisive action to go on the offensive.

There has been a seemingly endless stream of hatred directed toward President Bush from the beginning of the Iraq war, especially from those who believe there was no connection or association between al Qaeda and Iraq. To illustrate that such a belief is without basis in fact, I refer to Senate Joint Resolution 45, from the 107th Congress (which passed in the Senate with a vote of ninety-five to one). The following is a small sampling of the language of the resolution authorizing the president to use force against Iraq:

> "...the current Iraqi regime has demonstrated its capability and willingness to use weapons of mass destruction against other nations and its own people...members of al Qaeda, an organization bearing responsibility for attacks on the United States, its citizens, and interests, including the attacks that occurred on September 11, 2001, are known to be in Iraq...the attacks on the United States of September 11, 2001, underscored the gravity of the threat that Iraq will transfer weapons of mass destruction to international terrorist organizations."[26]

> "...Congress in the Iraq Liberation Act...has expressed its sense that it should be the policy of the United States to support efforts to remove from power the current Iraqi regime and promote the emergence of a democratic government to replace that regime...the President has authority under the Constitution to take action in order to deter and prevent acts of international terrorism against the United States...and...the President has authority under the Constitution to use force in order to defend the national security interests of the United States."[27]

"The president is authorized to use all means that he determines to be appropriate, including force, in order to enforce the United Nations Security Council Resolutions...defend the national security interests of the United States against the threat posed by Iraq, and restore international peace and security in the region."[28] The Senate of the United States sanctioned the president to use force in Iraq for regime change, among other things. The war in Iraq is not Bush's war, end of statement.

In a job I had as a general manager of a restaurant a Director of Operations often said to me and others that, "words mean things." What he meant by that is, don't say things you cannot support or that you do not believe to be true because there are always consequences. He was right. Each of us must accept the consequences of what we do or say, no matter what. The consequences of S.J. Resolution 45 was evidence that some of our Senators did not realize that their "words mean things." Some politicians do not like it when we remember their words and speak of holding them accountable.

Near the conclusion of the resolution it states, "We, the undersigned senators ... hereby move to bring to a close the debate on the motion to proceed to S.J. Res. 45 ... "[29] The date of this Cloture Motion was roughly five-and-a-half months prior to the beginning of the conflict in Iraq. One has to admit that the United States Senate must share responsibility as a partner in the war in Iraq, since it overwhelmingly passed a resolution authorizing the war, not to mention that no president can unilaterally enter into a conflict where U.S. Military forces will be involved without the blessing of Congressional approval. If questions or uncertainties about the intelligence existed, there was enough time that it could have been debated and discussed on the Senate floor before a final vote was rendered so that each member would have had absolutely no doubt about the meaning of a yes or no vote. Remember, the vote for a declaration of war in Iraq was a separate issue compared with the subject of how to initially fund the war, as well as ongoing funding.

It is stunning to note how incredibly arrogant human beings can be. With the information we possess about all the senators who voted to authorize the president to go into Iraq, I would like to explore some of the words of Senator John Kerry, spoken roughly ten months before the November 2004 presidential elections, of which Mr. Kerry was the eventual democratic nominee. Mr. Kerry appeared on *Meet the Press* with Tim Russert, with the obvious hope of increasing his stock among Iowa voters, as well as voters across the country.

Mr. Russert had asked the question about how much the senator's yes vote had damaged his standing with Iowa Democrats. It is amazing to examine how Mr. Kerry responded to that question. He said that the vote "was not a vote specifically to go to war; it was a vote to do what President Bush said he would do, which is hold Saddam Hussein accountable by going to the UN, working to build a legitimate global coalition, working to have an inspection process that was legitimate and that we were patient about, and finally, the president said he would go to war as a matter of last resort."[30] It is embarrassing that Mr. Kerry could actually make a statement that was so antithetical to his actual vote.

Unfortunately, like many of Mr. Kerry's colleague's politicians in this country have a problem with facts, as do some of the people who support them. And these same people must be under the mistaken belief that they can change the record any time they want if it is politically necessary to save face. And even then they often act as if they have the right to revise and extend their remarks, or whatever parliamentary procedures or rules they exercise while on the Congressional floor. The truth is that Senator Kerry, as well as nearly every other Senator voted for the authorization of force against Iraq and nothing he might say now or in the future can change that fact. I'm sorry that there are those who consider the pursuit of the truth as a personal attack.

Well, the great thing about Kerry's statement is that I have no desire to actually attack him personally, even though that is how some people will characterize my position. Mr. Kerry and many others like him perform an adequate amount of self-incrimination without help from me. I believe that we have an obligation to make sure that our fellow citizens are not apt to forget the words of our elected politicians, especially when they are so damning.

As a concerned American, I can merely act as a facilitator for fellow citizens, but I am ashamed by those who seemingly abdicate the rights we enjoy as a sovereign nation to protect and defend ourselves and the Constitution. Mr. Kerry asserted that we did not give enough time to the idea of developing a "legitimate global coalition." I have nothing against nations coming together in a broad coalition to defeat someone like Saddam Hussein. In the case of the "War on Terror," the United States, as a sovereign nation, does not need the approval of any other nation to defend itself, or go on the offensive against a group of cowardice killers. As a nation, we have lost the blood of too many people throughout the course of too many conflicts; we have invested some of the best blood since the days of the Revolution, fighting for the right to go on the offensive against any enemy that threatens to eradicate our way of life. Simply stated, there was too much at stake to give a tyrant like Saddam Hussein the upper hand; and anyone with the decency and intelligence knows it.

After the first Gulf War Saddam was supposedly bound by all UN Resolutions with respect to WMDs; specifically, that he be forthcoming to UN Weapons Inspectors as to the whereabouts of such weapons; and if he did not possess WMDs, that he would be accommodating with that information as well. So for John Kerry and anyone else to insist that our government was not "patient about" weapons inspections, is laughable, and is typical of what we get from many in the liberal establishment—say whatever you want with no fear of repercussion from the free press nor accountability to "we the people."

Since many liberals seem to rebel against facts, here's one from President Bush: "Recognizing the threat to our country, the United States Congress voted overwhelmingly ... to support the use of force against Iraq."[31] In addition, the president said that, "All the decades of deceit and cruelty have now reached an end. Saddam Hussein and his sons must leave Iraq within forty-eight hours. Their refusal to do so will result in military conflict, commenced at a time of our choosing."[32]

The resolution that Senator Kerry and ninety-four other senators passed was unmistakable in authorizing the president to use force in Iraq. Our country could no longer sit back on defense against one of the most aggressive enemy's this nation has ever known. Between the time of the Geneva Convention and the 1980's, enemies of the United States typically clad themselves in a uniform and were fairly recognizable, something quite different than an enemy like al Qaeda, which tend to try and blend in with those they attack.

With the advent of hate-filled, radical extremists, it would probably be wise to amend some of our outdated laws to reflect the evolved nature of all enemies, or potential enemies of the United States; but like any statute, it must be enforced if it is to mean anything. All I know is that neither the President nor Congress should ever be paralyzed because of the law. There have been laws made subsequent to the Constitution that might restrict the ability of elected leaders to make decisions which ultimately provide protection to American citizens. The president's primary role is to protect Americans from potentially harmful situations. Matters of war are challenging enough without a bunch of bureaucrats compounding issues under the guise of concern for protecting the civil liberties of the American people. I do not think we need a multitude of lawyers with time on their hands determining whether or not it is legal for the president (regardless of party) or Congress to defend this nation against its enemies.

Entering a conflict and putting American lives at stake requires strong leadership, not this: "I believed we needed to have Saddam Hussein held accountable. But you needed to do it right. And doing it right meant going through the United Nations properly, exhausting the remedies of the inspections. It meant taking the time to build a legitimate coalition, not a fraudulent one."[33] It would be difficult to qualify the weakness of John Kerry's leadership but it was never on greater display than after he made this statement. How many times did our government "do it right" by deferring to the U.N. during the many years dealing with Iraq since 1991? I am so tired of politicians who say the most outlandish things because they place their own selfish interests above the Constitution. The United States of America must never get into the habit of "going through the United Nations."

Democrats should not have been babbling to the press about how there was no connection between Iraq and al Qaeda; especially given the fact that their vote in Congress revealed a much different story. They certainly did their part to discredit George W. Bush. The outcome of Hussein's capture, trial and execution was a good thing for the rest of the world, and appears to have validated our involvement in Iraq. In addition, Hussein's sons, Uday and Qusay, received an even more prompt punishment in Mosul as they met their earthly fate at the hands of U.S. Forces.

When Mr. Russert challenged Senator Kerry about his admission to hold Saddam accountable, the senator explained: "We would be in Iraq if it—if we had exhausted the remedies of the inspections and Saddam Hussein had not complied. We would have used the legitimate threat of force."[34] The U.S. did exhaust "the remedies of the inspections," to the tune of about twelve years worth, to which Saddam failed to adequately comply. I suppose that the only acceptable use of legitimate force in Kerry's mind would have been anything but George W. Bush as Commander in Chief. The notion that somehow the U.S. did not have enough patience with Hussein or that the inspectors were not allowed enough time to do their job is preposterous and typical of some liberals. Is it any wonder that the senator from Massachusetts failed to become president of the United States?

Mr. Kerry learned the hard way and failed in his bid for the presidency. His efforts have rewarded him in his home state but let's hope that is as far as he ever gets. I will admit that there are times when the electorate seems to ignore factual information, which unfortunately ends up strengthening the emboldened politicians who continue to be awarded at the polls.

Finally, Tim Russert leveled a charge at Mr. Kerry concerning comments that he made regarding whether Howard Dean thought we were safer with Saddam captured or not:

> Mr. Russert: "Do you believe that Howard Dean does not have the judgment to be president or the credibility to be elected president?
>
> Senator Kerry: I think the judgment of a nominee who doesn't understand that having Saddam Hussein captured will make it extraordinarily difficult to be able to beat an incumbent wartime president who captured Saddam Hussein ... This is a man who has used weapons of mass destruction ... not only against other people but against his own people. This is a man who tried to assassinate a former president of the United States, a man who lobbed 36 missiles into Israel in order to destabilize the Middle East, a man who is so capable of miscalculation that he even brought this war on himself ... He would have continued to terrorize the people, just in their minds, because of thirty years of terror in Iraq."[35]

This incredible statement demonstrates Kerry's attempt to sound hawkish about the war. However, it is unbelievable. The mainstream press chose to ignore it. I find it amazing that just one week before the Iowa caucus Mr. Kerry willingly made a statement that forced him to try and defend the indefensible. It appears that he made such a statement in hopes of putting some distance between himself and the other democrats seeking to earn the nomination. Fortunately, the American people recognized his political expediency for what it was: an attempt to obtain the highest office in the land by saying what he thought he had to say at the time.

Time to fast forward post-inauguration of George W. Bush; John Kerry miraculously experienced a sudden, and I might add expected, epiphany with respect to the war in Iraq. Most people are painfully aware that a lot of politicians surmise that they can articulate and feign support for practically any position due to the level of apathy that exists among the general population in the country. Politicians are well aware that most Americans have a very short memory when it comes to remembering their personal blunders and indiscretions; indeed, most people in America seem to have a severely short attention span when it comes to politics. It seems to be too difficult for many Americans to take the time to be informed, and to make political choices based upon accurately acquired information.

Americans often place themselves over a barrel when it comes to the quality of some of our politicians. Where is the buyer beware placard warning us of potential hazards? Where is the guidebook telling us what we can expect relating to the quality of a politician? As a people, we should be able to expect that those whom we elect to office will be honest and forthright with their constituents; seems like a reasonable expectation. We have probably all experienced the same remorse when we decide on the cheaper priced item at the store or car lot because we convinced ourselves that we would be saving some hard-earned cash. I venture to say that we have all fallen prey to such dilemmas.

We sometimes experience the same dilemma when it comes to the politicians we elect; unfortunately, we usually get what we pay for, in a manner of speaking. We have all witnessed how candidates purport one thing on the campaign trail, then upon winning an election, morph into an entirely different type of person. We all need to remember the buyer beware philosophy when it comes time to cast our vote.

I recall in recent years that the approval rating for Congress slipped into the single digits. In fact, according to a Rasmussen Report "Just 9% say Congress is doing a good or excellent job."[36] I wonder if there were some voters around the country that may have felt as though they had been ripped off or short-changed. Fortunately, there is a remedy for such pitiful representation; the beauty of politics in America. We are really never in a situation where we have to just take what we get. Every few years, we have the privilege of going to the polls and firing the people who have failed to be accountable to us. Unfortunately for members of the U.S. House, that opportunity comes around every two years. It is interesting to note the often dismal approval ratings of both the Legislative as well as the Executive branches of government during the Bush Administration, which did not necessarily bode well for either party.

FANNIE AND FREDDIE REVISITED; CHARACTER OF THOSE IN THE KNOW

I believe that politicians and others associated with Fannie and Freddie benefited by the fact that there were too many other "distractions" going on at the time of the downfall of these two companies; not to mention the horrendous condition they were in because of inattention given to the two enormous GSEs by politicians in years past. By the time the sub-prime mortgage situation reached a boil, the country was in the midst of an economic downturn, not to mention the presidential election between Barack Obama and John McCain. Naturally, the candidates were probably very anxious to leave the Senate behind given the dismal approval ratings. With so much evidence seemingly pointing to the democrats as the party most complicit in the Fannie and Freddie messes, Senator McCain could have done more to expose democrats, including Mr. Obama, since he was running for the highest office in the land. The opportunity to expose allegations against those involved in the scandal as the slime of the earth may have been lost for good. It is unconscionable and pathetic to fathom that anyone associated with illegal activity like stealing money from companies that were supposed to be in the business of helping the very people that liberal politicians tend to court.

We cannot talk about the Fannie and Freddie mess without talking about the Clinton administration. I actually wish that

Clinton would fade away into private life. Of all the living ex-presidents, there has probably never been one who has sought the limelight and approval of the public more than Clinton, despite competition from Jimmy Carter. I would hope that most people would be perfectly content to let both of these former presidents sink into the oblivion of retirement—go fishing, golfing, or whatever; eliminate world hunger; just go and do all the things to eliminate suffering that they seem to think liberalism is supposed to cure.

The Clinton administration was not only on the bandwagon for Fannie and Freddie but also led the charge to ensure that banks ended up making risky loans to people who they knew would most likely not be credit worthy. I suppose we could say that home ownership qualifies as a "pursuit of happiness" in America, but not necessarily a right. There is no shame in renting a home until improved financial circumstances make it possible to take on a mortgage. By attempting to take on more than they can handle, Americans run the risk of damaging their credit, which ends up being no good for all concerned parties. The whole credit issue relating to the sub-prime market is just another example of how some politicians knowingly mislead the public in hopes of garnering votes. So why does there seem to be no real effort to go after the crooks who are behind the Fannie and Freddie scandals? I can only hope that concrete steps will be taken to prosecute these people to the fullest extent of the law. But being acquainted with the infrequent nature of prosecuting political crooks, I have my doubts that anything will actually ever happen.

Fortunately, for those who are involved in the many scandals that seem to never end, there is always generally plenty of distractions to keep people from focusing on something like Fannie Mae and Freddie Mac, or a host of other things. The government, regardless of conservative or liberal label, should have taken advantage of the opportunity to take people to task over the charade at Fannie and Freddie when it was still a hot-button issue because it would have been the right thing to do. Regrettably, I suspect that it may now be too late. In an article linking the falsification of signatures to Fannie Mae bonuses written by Kathleen Day and Terence O'Hara , they state: "Fannie Mae reported paying the following executive bonuses in 1998: chairman and chief executive James A. Johnson received $1.932 million; Franklin D. Raines, chairman-designate, received $1.11 million; Chief Operating Officer Lawrence M. Small received $1.108 million; Vice Chairman Jamie S. Gorelick received $779,625; Chief Financial Officer J. Timothy Howard received $493,750; and Robert J. Levin, an executive vice president, received $493,750."[37] This all took place under the Clinton administration. How could such exorbitant bonuses have been paid at a time when people were losing their homes?

Amazingly, there are those that may be inclined to defend people who get something for nothing; most average Americans, however, probably do not share the same sentiment. How can executives at any company reap huge benefits from bonuses that are based on false accounting numbers? Perhaps the most incredible facet of this story is the seeming lack of outrage by a majority of Americans. The average person should be totally outraged at these findings, if only they took the time to be informed; because the average American does not make anywhere near the money that rivals even the minimum bonus amount received by these executives. And it is not even that most people have a problem with the amount of money someone is able to earn; provided it is legitimately earned!

Seriously, what could you do if you received $493,750 in the form of a bonus above and beyond your regular salary? Getting a bonus from a company that was going down the toilet is about as obscene as it gets, please! I am wholeheartedly in support of free markets and capitalism; but those who are guilty of scamming from Fannie while pretending that the window display was an accurate portrayal of what was going on inside must be held to account for their actions. Attempting to pass off as legitimate a reward for hard work and effort when it was anything but legitimate capitalism should never go unpunished.

I suppose there will also be those who may claim that someone like Franklin Raines has paid his debt to society by shelling out more than $24 million to federal regulators in exchange for charges being dropped; however, I guess I'm "old school." As I understand it, if you break the law, serving time behind bars is designed to compel remorse, at least until genuine remorse is attained; and then to impose punishment which will hopefully support the rehabilitation process. There is something about losing the freedom to come and go that usually has a tendency to reform those who are truly sorry for the crimes they have committed. Getting a slap on the wrist and paying a fine just does not seem adequate.

It is probably impossible for a CEO to know every single detail happening in a company, be it financial or otherwise. But considering the extraordinary compensation packages of today's CEO, it ought to be common sense that as the CEO of a large organization, it would probably be pertinent to know whether the boatload of money deposited into your bank account was earned legitimately; just in case a really bored federal regulator shows up asking for justification of your manipulated, over-the-top, and extremely fat bonus. It seems to me that the mere fact that charges had been pending against Mr. Raines and that he was given the option of making such a huge "payoff" to make things right...well, seems a little suspicious. Most of us are aware that money tends to corrupt those with little or no discipline; however, I still believe that the majority of hard-working, decent Americans would not accept a big payoff for doing something that is illegal. I'm an optimist.

It seems to me that those who make their living as prosecutors would have little difficulty finding evidence that Mr. Raines knew of the book-cooking buffet taking place at Fannie. Both Mr. Johnson and Mr. Raines, followed by a host of evidently eager people, stepped right up to the head of the line with bank account numbers at the ready. It did not seem to matter that the people who are "supposed" to care were aware that many of the people entering into sub-prime loans would eventually be stuck with mortgages that they could not handle. Instead of giving these folks access to taxpayer dollars, we should just round up all the people who received bonuses based on phony numbers, and use those funds to bail out the holders of delinquent loans. That does not negate the fact that loans were entered into prematurely, but it seems better than strapping taxpayers with the burden. The bottom line is that most of the people who entered into sub-prime loans knew of their personal financial situation better than any lender, so obviously accountability is not just a problem restricted to CEOs and elected politicians.

There were obviously many people culpable for what was happening at Fannie and Freddie, inside the company and in Congress as well. Where is the public outcry with this case, similar to what we witnessed during the Enron debacle? Books were falsified at Enron to make shareholders believe that the company was in better financial condition than in all actuality. I fail to see how what happened at Fannie Mae is any different than what took place at Enron. After an investigation of Enron, evidence was gathered and indictments followed; most people would agree that prosecution was swift and punishment meted out in the case, except for those unfortunate enough to have been counting on an Enron nest egg for retirement. Will we ever see those punished in the Fannie case that is remotely comparable to what we witnessed of those involved in the Enron case? Time will tell. I do not recall what type of settlement was reached for shareholders at Enron; however, my guess is that it was nothing compared to what it might have been otherwise.

There seems to be much less concern about what happened to GSEs like Fannie and Freddie, I suppose because there are so many in the government who were neck deep in the scandal. Looking at Enron or any of the other notable companies in the early part of the twenty-first century that had major accounting problems, all of them had a horrible ending for a lot of people. Usually every private company accepts the reality of success or failure and the risks associated with it, that the only guarantee is the opportunity to try. But GSEs like Fannie Mae and Freddie Mac, backed by the full faith and credit of the United States government (you and me) get to continue beyond failure under a supposedly even more stringent government plan called conservatorship. Raines and his cronies dressed up earnings so that they could pretend to qualify for outrageous bonuses. Unbelievably, Mr. Raines, writing an editorial article in the *Wall Street Journal,* had this to say:

> "Shame on you. The *Wall Street Journal,* of all publications, has the opportunity and responsibility to provide leadership ... Unfortunately, in your ... editorial about Fannie Mae, you only fan fears with your glib, disingenuous, contorted, even irresponsible attempt to tar our company with the Enron brush. At best, the editorial betrays a complete lack of knowledge or understanding about our business. At worst, you chose the thrill of a good smear job over the hard work of reporting or writing opinion pieces grounded in facts."[38]

We can only presume that Mr. Raines is speaking from experience. I agree that there were a lot of people who had "a complete lack of knowledge or understanding" about what you were actually doing at Fannie. I find it disturbing that Mr. Raines was critical of an editorial comparing similar improprieties of the company he was in charge of, to that of Enron. The contempt exhibited is typical of one who knows he did wrong. It is interesting to note that Mr. Raines's editorial is at, or near the end of his tenure with Fannie Mae; at a time when he was fully aware of what he had presided over, all under his watchful eye, and all taking place with his approval.

It is simply unbelievable that at the time Mr. Raines was writing his editorial in the *Wall Street Journal,* that he had no idea of the financial travesty going on at Fannie Mae. Can there be any doubt that we are neck deep in a culture of corruption in America today, even if it is a relatively small percentage of people who cast a shadow over capitalism or politics? It is a problem that needs to be rectified, but not necessarily by Washington. It usually only takes a few bad apples to ruin it for everyone else, which seems to motivate politicians to want a piece of the action, since many elected politicians are unaccustomed with the functionality of capitalism. A lot of politicians and people like Mr. Raines must think that the American people are a bunch of cretins; I imagine that we are not as idiotic as they oftentimes probably hope. I also submit that members of Congress who had their tentacles all over Fannie and Freddie are not as stupid as some may think. There are some very crafty people in the halls of Congress, many of whom have become adept at artful forms of manipulation. It seems that the reason for the lack of accountability from within Congress is due to the fact that no one wants to implicate a colleague, whether in the Fannie/Freddie scandals or any number of situations that "we the people" are often not even aware of. How much more evidence do we need that members of Congress are actually part of a very elite fraternity where behavior is often reprehensible and accountability to the people is seemingly ignored or simply forgotten? We tend not to accept it in the private sector, so why should we accept it from our elected representatives?

I realize that there have been tons of books and articles written on the subject of the quality of those elected to represent the people. I also understand that practically nothing has been done to stem the tide of unscrupulous people making their way onto the political stage. I am amazed that some of these people get elected in the first place. The difficulties associated with keeping less-than-desirable folks from seeking public office are daunting; and it appears that it is even more so for the people who actually vote for them. One of the reasons that make the process difficult is the fact that it does not take political office seekers very long to realize that the trick is saying whatever you have to say to appease the people and get yourself elected the first time. Once the door to the fraternity is cracked, access is granted to practically anything, and becoming a card carrying member with a sweet retirement is what you can look forward to receiving. If by chance re-election is denied, the joy of an incredible pension for life will still be yours, regardless of how long or how well you may have served. Career-minded politicians learn very quickly how to amass as much money as possible by being impressive enough to fool just enough of the electorate every election cycle; not exactly emblematic of a representative republic.

People in politics, and other notoriously popular individuals should also be careful because they never know when a camera may be rolling to record their ill-conceived remarks, or in the case of Franklin Raines where his words in a newspaper article didn't exactly leave positive lasting impressions of himself. Ask George Allen or Vice President Joe Biden about their experiences with foot and mouth disease. Unfortunately for Mr. Allen, his voting constituency had a different set of values regarding his hopes of being re-elected to the U.S. Senate. He lost his reelection bid; at least in part because he used a derogatory term "(macaca)"to characterize an individual listening to him speak. Clearly the same principles have not applied in Mr. Biden's case. My guess is that Allen's method is not the way to win constituents and influence voters; not to mention its inappropriate, demeaning, and abrasive tone even if it had not been picked up for the rest of the world to see and hear. But happy days! If you happen to be a democrat feel free to say to anyone who will listen that when you walk into a 7-Eleven or Dunkin' Donuts, like in Joe Biden's neck of the woods, it helps if you have a "slight Indian accent."[39] I cannot even begin to defend either one of these idiotic comments. However, my point is that the Democratic Party in America seems to get a pass when it comes to these kinds of comments; and in the case of Joe Biden, people simply justify it by acknowledging that it is just Joe being Joe. How pathetically repulsive!

There seems to be more emphasis on outward appearance than on substance, which unfortunately is prevalent across much of our society, not just politics. Sadly, ignorant people have a lot of influence in American politics today; a risk that our system of government must endure. The people of this country should take the time to be informed in order to overcome ignorance. Obviously, the media could do so much more to disseminate information to the people in an unbiased manner so that people can make up their own minds.

POLITICIANS, PEOPLE, MEDIA: SOME ISSUES

As a conservative, I believe that there are deep and abiding philosophical differences that exists between the two major parties; however, in the more than twenty years since Reagan left office, many conservatives in the Republican Party seem to have lost the will to courageously articulate those differences, in order to remain distinguishable from the Democratic Party. For instance, during the eight years that George W. Bush was president, we had a "conservative" in office that did not seem to like using the veto pen to limit wasteful spending, something that has traditionally been a major point of contrast to typical liberal fiscal philosophy. Perhaps Forty-Three kept hoping that liberals would be more sympathetic toward him if he made no real attempt to limit spending. We all know how that turned out. Unfortunately, Bush strayed from core conservative principles and all it seemed to accomplish was to build the foundation for Obama to coast into office. Upon his arrival, he signed another huge bailout bill, laden with special interest pork and so-called earmarks, even though Obama claims there was no pork in the bill. And he did this all within the first ninety days of his presidency after he had campaigned against such spending, with the reasoning, at least in part due to the belief that companies were too big to fail.

Most people who care deeply about all things political often profess their steadfast allegiance to a particular party; personally, I believe in the precepts of conservatism first; party affiliation is secondary. We can never forget that the mainstream media always tend to align with democrats, no matter what they attempt to profess. The traditional media portrayal of conservatism seems to be the way many people view all conservatives: white, male, rich, suburban-dwelling, heartland living, homophobic, religious fanatic, gun toting, narrow minded, unfair, anti-immigration and anti-progressive! It is inaccurate to portray conservatism in this manner; just as it is unfair to portray liberals by many of the stereotypical labels that carelessly get tossed around to describe them by those not associated with the mainstream media. For the best analysis on mainstream media predisposition to liberals, Bernard Goldberg's *Bias* is a must read. So in the last several years, when it comes to fiscal responsibility, neither conservatives nor liberals (not that we would expect it) seem willing to take the lead to reign in out-of-control spending of the taxpayers' money.

As a conservative, I *want* there to be undeniable differences between democrats and republicans; though most conservatives vote republican, many republicans such as Lindsey Graham and John McCain do not demonstrate the kind of consistent conservative principles that are necessary. I am tired of glassy-eyed, power hungry politicians constantly running their mouths but saying nothing at all; except whatever they believe to be politically expedient. This type of behavior is most exemplified during a campaign, making it that much more difficult for the people to know who they should support.

I do not want people like former Republican Senator Arlen Specter, whose defection to the Democratic Party resulted from a belief that his chances for re-election as a republican, seemingly based on a poll, were extremely slim. Real core conservative stance there, huh? As a matter-of-fact, Mr. Specter said, "I am unwilling to have my twenty-nine year senate record judged by the Pennsylvania Republican primary electorate."[40] News flash Mr. Specter: That's how it's supposed to work—that's why we call it a representative republic; the people get to decide if you are doing the job they elected you to do! Just because Specter suspected that he might get defeated in an upcoming primary because of what the polls may have projected; he should have had the decency and integrity not to abandon his party or principle.

Specter is a man who typifies many of the current breed in Washington that believe that the rest of us cannot possibly get along without their benevolence; and that because of time in office, they somehow have earned the right to remain permanent fixtures; much like many of the statues erected in Washington to honor the greatness of past leaders like Lincoln and Jefferson. Well, it is obvious that Mr. Specter did conservatives a huge favor by switching parties, as most people were well aware of his lack of commitment to conservatism in the first place. So even though I am not completely happy with the state of the conservative movement, I am glad that a republican in name only (RINO) like Specter is no longer a member of the GOP.

It seems obvious to the perceptive that the mainstream media do a really good job trying to persuade "we the people" to support liberals. The funny thing about the mainstream media is that they all know how they treat conservatism, yet they continue to pretend that they possess objectivity when challenged by anyone accusing them of partiality. However, "we the people" do not have to be dependent on ABC, CBS, and NBC to spoon feed us anymore; not to mention the other cable outlets combined never seem to attract as many viewers as even one of the popular FOX News programs in prime time. It is interesting that some of the people in the media enjoy promoting freedom of speech when it is in line with their personal beliefs. But wait until a conservative, for instance, expresses a viewpoint that is in direct conflict with what they believe; then the right to speak freely suddenly becomes a big deal. It is amazing that the "big three" networks have managed to last as long as they have.

What is even more amazing is that they and their supporters whine about how biased FOX News is toward conservatism.

The mainstream media must be held to account for what they do on a daily basis, not just the egregious attempts to malign conservatism. Their nefarious objectives must be exposed for what they are: a shameless attempt to promote anything that's not conservative. Alternatives to the mainstream media were a long time in coming; however, I imagine the "big three" have cursed the day that cable, talk radio, and not the least of which, FOX News, rained on their parade.

I have mentioned my belief that there are still differences between the two major political parties in America, even though both have enjoyed spending sprees that rival hardened shopaholics. The problem with conservatism is that there have not been enough people with the guts to tell it like it is and let the chips fall where they may. The elites in office, regardless of party, are too concerned about maintaining the power of their office, especially when there's an election on the horizon. I realize that each party has a platform and that there are key issues associated with a particular platform; that there is a much talked about fringe faction associated with the conservative and liberal wings of each party.

For instance, democrats typically support high tax rates, greater control over the lives of "we the people," abortion (now cleverly coined as women's health issues or a woman's right to choose), less spending on defense and fiddling with raising the minimum wage (as if that is going to be the impetuous for creating the next batch of millionaires). Republicans typically favor lower taxes for all who pay them, less government control in the lives of "we the people," a pro-life stance, strong defense spending in support of our military, and lower overall government spending. There was a time when the lines were pretty clearly drawn between democrats and republicans relative to spending. It seemed that over the last few years of Bush's presidency, and when republicans had control in Congress; they failed to clearly distinguish themselves from their spend-happy brethren. That philosophy must change and then remain as a distinguishable characteristic when pointing out differences between the two, especially if republicans want to be the majority party in congress. Sure it would be great if there was complete agreement on every political issue, but as far as I know, that has never happened, so it's probably not an option. Certainly, the health care debate has done much to open the eyes of the people regarding the spending philosophies of the two major political parties, and perhaps going forward it will be motivation for conservatives to further distinguish themselves generally from the spending habits of liberals.

I realize that since the formation of the Republic, there have been divisions created by people self-identifying, or having had a particular label attached by virtue of a particular ideology; such as conservative or liberal. I find it ironic that most elected liberals seem to choose not to identify themselves as liberal even though many of their constituents readily accept the label. I suppose a more commonly used term, but really no different in terms of philosophy for liberals today is progressivism. In either case many people are beginning to understand the nature of government dependency preached from the pulpit of liberalism or progressivism. On the other side most conservatives usually have no problem describing themselves as conservative, unless they have been elected to public office, as there are those who lack the will to promote conservative ideals for fear that they might be singled out as uncaring or insensitive. When was the last time you heard an elected leader extol the virtues of liberalism or talk about the overwhelming pride they experience as a liberal? Or since the health care debate began raging, I don't recall too many liberals attempting to articulate the details and benefits of government controlled health care, only that it will be better if it's mandated by the government. By the same token, it does not seem all that common for elected conservatives to regularly commend the soundness of conservative ideals. Where are the conservatives who supported keeping health care privatized and who suggested that all the entities involved in the health care industry come together to work out a plan that would be viable for all consumers of health care, instead of relying on the government to put their control-hungry hands all over it? As far as I'm concerned, no conservative who has been a member of Congress over the last couple of decades, who has not made an effort to get wasteful spending under control, has no right to lecture us about the need for health care insurance reform. A lot of liberals who support some sort of government run health care have no problem, for instance, pointing out how often private insurance seems to deny claims. Perhaps those same people may need to look into how often Medicare denies a claim for a healthy dose of perspective; not to mention the difficulties associated with the red tape appeals process when pursuing a denied claim.

I do not mind being labeled as a conservative since that is what I profess. I just want to be able to articulate those views and have them respected even though they may not be agreed with. I know what I stand for and it is my hope that all who read this book will have a better understanding of the direction I believe conservatism ought to go.

Some labels are even more destructive than either conservative or liberal and they often seem to have a tendency to divide people in a way that is not necessary because of the focus on superficial characterizations, like skin color, gender, and looks, which often prevent us from finding common ground. There are honest differences between conservatives and liberals, which can be discussed and debated in a civil fashion. It seems to me that if things are to get better for the people, their representatives must figure out a way to govern in a civil manner, even when there is disagreement. We should not look the other way in cases of impropriety with respect to our elected officials; elections have consequences and words have meaning. We cannot continue to accept business as usual or that it's just "politics."

Elections are getting ridiculous when candidates cannot even point out legitimate discrepancies about an opponent's policies or questionable character issues without being labeled as attacking the individual. Once again, the media need to be accountable to the people for reporting objectively and getting it right; we do not want to hear the personal opinions and the subjectivism that often are a big part of the news; we just need the people who are paid to report the news to focus on that and not actually do what they can to create *news*. Please do not be confused by what is said on the *news*, compared to what is said on the cable "opinion" shows. The news is supposed to be reported without bias. The opinion shows are just that, predominantly the opinion of the host. Obviously, opinion shows will be blatantly skewed to reflect the personal bias of the host, and will naturally be disproportionate when compared to the news. That's the way it is and it does not mean that those who are supposed to report the news are at liberty to take the same approach. Talk radio and certain cable shows are not equivalent to the news, especially since the owners and operators of radio stations and cable outlets that carry talk shows are at liberty to market whatever brand they believe will bring in the best revenue. Here again, if liberals have their way they will also have control of every other aspect of the free market.

The conflict continues between conservatism and liberalism. Perhaps we may some day witness the formation of a formidable third party once again in American politics. However, it is unlikely given that in order for something like a third party to work, the philosophies of a third party would have to be drastically different than what we now have. Somehow, I do not see that happening any time soon. And even though moderates may pose a drastic difference to both liberalism and conservatism, I do not believe such a philosophy to be the foundation of a formidable third party. Ultimately, a major third party would have to be something more than the same old stuff bottled up in a different package, with a few modifications.

Third party attempts at the general election level have been tried in recent years and all that usually ends up happening is that a slim percentage of the vote is taken away from Democratic or Republican candidates. Seriously, a democrat-turned-independent like Joe Lieberman still caucuses with the democrats even though the democrats have routinely turned on him since his defection. So what good is the independent label? What we need are candidates from either party who are committed to serving the people. Candidates must not take themselves too seriously and actually do that which will show the people of their willingness to serve them, while maintaining a sense of respect and decorum for the political process. That does not mean that candidates capitulate when it comes to principled beliefs.

Bringing an end to the power of some of our entrenched politicians is a good idea; and even though our two-party system has had challenges since Lincoln, I believe that the best deterrent to unmitigated power and control is responsible governance, because when practiced, it has worked for centuries; the people should be at liberty to control their own future as opposed to having it controlled for them by the government. Barack Obama promised to change things for the people; make things more transparent. Well, he has sure changed things and it is appropriate to question how that change has been working out. The newness has definitely faded to something that is even far worse than "business as usual" in Washington. Unfortunately, we are just getting more of the tax-and-spend liberal philosophy running the show at nearly every turn. I suppose we are simply getting what Colin Powell says we want: "Americans ... looking for more government in their life, not less."[41]

One could make the argument that the mainstream media itself has become somewhat of a third party; if not for the fact that there is more favorable treatment of democrats compared to republicans, that statement might have some truth to it. Oftentimes, the media act as if they are literally involved in shaping public policy; and to some extent, they seem to be having a lot of success because they are the masters of *spin*. The media realize the considerable weight it carries and the powerful influence it has over the public. There are probably still a lot of regular folks that swear by the mainstream press; though, gone are the iconic figures that used to have such amazing control over the people because of that which they called trust. Many Americans most likely trust very little of what they hear from the mainstream media. Where would we be today without the advent of talk radio and other sources of information? It is time to take a look at some examples of what I have been talking about regarding the media and their deference to liberals.

During the 2008 presidential campaign it was interesting to see how much emphasis the mainstream media put on Governor Sarah Palin, not necessarily because it favored her. There seemed to be more negative emphasis and interest on the fact that $150,000 was spent to supply the governor with a new wardrobe than on matters of quite a bit more significance. Where was the media when it came to investigating the questionable relationships of radical people to Senator Obama? Like most things, they pretended to give the topic coverage and were too busy to concern themselves and just gave him a pass after demonizing anyone who brought up the topic of questionable relationships. Not surprising, we were brainwashed by the media in the 1990s into believing that the personal relationships that the president (or one who hopes to become president) has in his private life do not affect his ability to govern. How about this doozie from the late Representative John Murtha just days after referring to people as racist in Western Pennsylvania: "What I said, that indicted everybody, that's not what I meant at all [The famous *that's not what I meant* line followed by the real meaning]. What I meant is there's still folks that have a problem voting for someone because they are black... this whole area, years ago, was really redneck"[42] (emphasis added). Unbelievable! We all know that if Murtha had an (R) after his name instead of a (D) that the media would have never let the public forget such a poorly stated correction, let alone the first blunder. Need proof? Look no further than George Allen (R), and macaca. I guess rednecks are generally perceived as "white," so apparently a comment like Murtha's makes it acceptable.

This business of preferred party politicians using the media as an extension of their staff is getting to be a bit old. The media seem to enjoy reporting the things that they want the people to believe because they seldom condemn their favored party, even when it appears in the case of Murtha, someone handed him a ladder and said: *We know you will make a ridiculous comment today, so you will need this to get out of the humongous hole you'll be in later.* Of course, the hole and the ladder are contingent on the media doing the right thing by actually reporting objectively and letting the people who may be watching form their own assessments. It is pitiful to witness tired, worn-out statements like: "That is not what I meant," that so many politicians seem to believe they can rely on in the event their foot gets anywhere near their mouth. What I am about to say is complete conjecture on my part, but it seems to me that many of the elites consciously think that if they say something completely stupid or foolish today, they can just go back out in front of the microphones afterward and pull out their trump card or idiot disclaimer form and smooth things over. Perhaps the most stunning thing about the Murtha incident during the 2008 campaign season is that he managed to get himself re-elected to another term in the United States Congress; but of course, the media had nothing to do with that.

We should now be able to put to rest the silly idea that it does not matter what derogatory blather comes out of the mouth of a person when running for office. It seems all that is required to be qualified to apologize for foot and mouth disease is to be so believable that even your granny would believe you. And that big (D) behind your name certainly doesn't hurt.

We have to wonder about the charade that has become the "freedom" of the press. I am convinced that the politicians who pull the kind of stunts that would get them fired in the private sector regard the grand scheme of things in their warped little world as nothing more than a game to see how much they can get away with; and I might add that for some career politicians, their winning percentage is quite good. I mean, where else can you use phrases like "That is not what I meant," or "I apologize," in perpetuity with no consequences? It is reminiscent of Walt Disney's *Pinocchio*.[43]

In this timeless classic, there is a segment where Pinocchio and Jiminy Cricket get on a boat and travel to Treasure Island with a bunch of unsuspecting boys with the intent to live it up, have some fun, and do whatever they want to do without accepting any responsibility for their actions. Unbeknownst to Pinocchio and his human counterparts, they do not realize that the place they are actually going is a place where "stupid boys" go who like to play hooky from school. While on Treasure Island, they meet up with a boy named Lampwick who ultimately gets turned into a jackass with the rest of his irresponsible, derelict buddies. Incidentally, I wonder if there is any correlation to the way the boys on Treasure Island behave in *Pinocchio* and the way some of our politicians behave in Washington, D.C. Well, no matter, though it does seem that a lot of politicians are living it up on Treasure Island, thinking that they will never have to grow up and take responsibility for their actions. It is a great blessing that we can get rid of those who have failed to live up to promises made to represent the interests of the people and be responsible.

Dealing with the media can be slightly more difficult than deciding what to do about a derelict politician. "We the people" do not have the authority to dismiss irresponsible behavior in the media quite as easily as booting bad behavior in politics. However, we do have the ability to choose not to support those in the media that make every effort to consistently and unapologetically report irresponsibly. Informed Americans, in an attempt to end careless reporting, must hit these people where it counts; in the ratings. With so many talk radio shows and cable options, there is no reason that anyone should feel obligated to obtain information by those who would rather force people to conform to their narrow point-of-view.

The mainstream media in this country have shown their true colors by demonizing folks like Ann Coulter, Larry Elder, Rush Limbaugh, Sean Hannity, Mark Levin, and Glenn Beck because they perceive them to be a threat to their warped school of thought. However, that does not give them the right to advocate measures to silence their First Amendment rights, especially since the aforementioned individuals are not responsible for reporting the news. The mainstream media often label anyone whose philosophy is different than liberalism as someone who is controversial, instead of someone who is provocative. Could it be that people like Katie Couric and David Gregory cannot begin to fathom the idea that they could actually be considered controversial? People like these two seem to truly believe that only conservative values can be considered controversial in America today.

Conservatives are made to feel as if they are the ones that need to be more tolerant and accepting of liberalism, and the mainstream media are only too willing to play along. It is my belief, generally speaking, that conservatives have not done enough to educate the public on the values of conservatism, especially knowing what they are up against. I am talking about everyday, run-of-the-mill conservatives who could have a greater impact for good in the conservative movement because of daily associations with those who do not now appreciate conservatism. For instance, we need to take the time to educate our fellow human beings on the virtues of self-reliance, a major thread of conservatism. People need to know the importance of individual responsibility and contributing to society. Oftentimes, the more liberal notion of governmental reliance, coupled with irresponsible behavior is rewarded with additional benefits from the government (taxpayers); which only serves to foster greater dependence upon government, the bedrock of liberalism.

THE POISON OF POLITICS

It has become nearly taboo for Americans to speak out about the need for individual responsibility since such a philosophy often differs with that of liberalism. Let's take a look at the subject of abortion as a *right,* for instance; contrasted with the importance of personal responsibility, thus pre-empting the need for many abortions in the first place. It seems that there are those who appear to be too afraid to teach correct principles and the tremendous responsibility required of two people engaged in an activity, which begins the process for bringing another human life into existence. I know that it is probably considered by many to be mean and old fashioned of me to put forth the idea that one of the most intimate of human experiences ought to be controlled, and most enjoyed within a prescribed bond.

Many people engage in a sexual relationship before they are in a position to be committed to everything else. Some people will question what right I have to speak out in denying the pleasures of life to anyone who wants a sexual relationship. It is my belief, whether it is popular or not, to teach sexual abstinence prior to a committed relationship (marriage). People who make the choice to have children only after marriage are often ridiculed and scorned in our culture as being oddballs for not giving in to the temptation to have sex. Incorrect moral behavior cannot be justified simply because it is practiced by a majority of the people.

There are instances when the life of the mother is threatened unless an abortion is performed, in such rare instances a difficult decision must be made based upon the people involved in such a dilemma. I would not impose my personal beliefs or render judgment upon anyone forced to make a decision to choose between one who is living, over the life of the unborn. I'm not a doctor, however, it would seem that there are probably relatively few circumstances that warrant an abortion to save the life of the mother, but that does not make the decision any easier. It would seem that the life of the mother would outweigh the life of an unborn child, especially if such a mother has dependent children. I would not want to have to make such an agonizing decision.

The dilemma of abortion should probably bring into question the personal moral behavior of people living outside the marriage vow, which tends to be a touchy subject to address. If personal behavior cannot be "legislated," then why did abortion find its way into the moral conscientiousness of Americans to the degree that it has? It would seem that as Americans, we are content to have allowed nine politically appointed judges to make the decision for us as opposed to allowing the people to make the choice with respect to the legalization of abortion. Though I may disagree with the outcome, the democratic thing to do is to let the States decide the "legality" of abortion by putting it on a ballot so that the people can exercise their rights. Instead, in America we have taken perhaps the most illogical step in justifying, not exclusively, often promiscuous behavior by legislating against those incapable of making the decision to enter mortality on their own. I understand that the topic of abortion is very personal; often one in which mainstream American politics refuses to explore because they're content with *Roe vs. Wade* as it is. Perhaps adherence to a higher law would negate the necessity for the legal process that has ended the lives of countless millions since 1973.

Anyone familiar with the presidential campaigns of 2008 recognized that the media seemed to have an obvious affinity for the Obama/Biden ticket. That is not necessarily a bad thing; however, it is when various members of the same media did not seem to devote a similar amount of quality time and affection to the McCain/Palin ticket. It is especially troubling since many of those same elite media had gone gaga for Senator McCain during the Republican primaries of 2000. It seems pretty clear there is an insatiable desire among the media to try and sway the outcome of the public to suit their agenda. Naturally, those whom the media favors so highly (liberals) feign shock and disbelief that the media are in their hip pocket; perhaps that is why those same people become so defensive whenever such an assertion of bias is made. But it is difficult to dispute the truth.

I want to point out the utter hypocrisy as evidenced by some in the media toward those who do not measure up to their idea of "progressive." Let it be understood that I use media as a generic term applicable to anyone who writes or speaks to the masses.

In September 2006, Katie Couric began her career in the anchor's chair at CBS News; which seems to be demonstrative of how the playing field is being leveled, and clearly opened the way for Ms. Couric to be subjected to the same kind of criticism often only reserved for her male peers. Couric should not be judged any differently just because she is a female; she should be subjected to the same scrutiny as her male peers with regard to her ability and merit as a journalist, not on whether her outfit is unbecoming or her eye shadow the wrong color. Feminists' refer to the hope of being judged by the same criteria used to evaluate a man's performance as equal rights; yet it seems to have exceeded even that, given the fact that Couric makes more money than most males who perform similar tasks while on the job. I could care less; more power to Couric for being able to command such a high salary. In an article written by Lauren Stiller Rikleen entitled "Women need Katie Couric to Succeed," Ms. Rikleen makes some very interesting statements.

Rikleen asserts that, "Study after study demonstrates that women are evaluated more harshly than men and that unconscious stereotyping creates far greater hurdles for women seeking to advance in the workplace."[44] I do not doubt that this is true. We live in a society dominated by males. My point in making this assessment is not to focus attention on the plight of Katie Couric making her debut on CBS News. Rather, my objective is to point out the obvious: that only certain females deserve to be defended by other females, or anyone else for that matter. Did Ms. Rikleen make the same effort to defend Governor Sarah Palin, for instance, during the 2008 presidential campaign? Granted, Ms Rikleen's article was written in September

2006, which should have given her plenty of time to prepare for someone like Sarah Palin. What are we to assume for her apparent lack of focus to write in support of Governor Palin? It is possible that she has written something in support of the governor, unbeknownst to me. If that is the case, I apologize for my lack of research. At any rate here is another one of Rikleen's statements: "As Katie Couric strives to succeed in what has been a distinctly male domain, women should be rooting for her success. She is undertaking a highly visible role where the examination will be relentless."[45]

This is really wonderful. I applaud Ms. Rikleen's support for Katie Couric and the hope that she succeed. However, if there has ever been a more male dominated domain than the U.S. Presidency and Vice Presidency, I'm all ears. From the days of the founding fathers, we have never had a woman nominated by her party to be president, nor have we had a woman chosen as a vice presidential running mate prior to Geraldine Farraro in 1984. And then twenty-four years later John McCain selected Governor Sarah Palin, the second woman ever to be selected to such a position. It seems to me that Rikleen and her concern for the apparent lack of opportunities for women to "get ahead" in society should have been jumping for joy to promote Governor Palin in every way possible, irrespective of such petty labels like republican or conservative.

Finally, Ms. Rikleen had this to say about Ms. Couric: "[And] she deserves some time to find that comfort zone. If she can successfully navigate the anticipated gauntlet of scrutiny and ultimately be judged on her competence, she will make it easier for other women who seek to break through gender barriers and be evaluated on their job performance ... Katie Couric can be expected to handle the glare with grace. That quality will serve as a positive role model for women everywhere who are striving to succeed in unfamiliar territory. Women need this success story to have a happy ending."[46] I do not know everything that has been written about the significance of Senator

McCain's choice of Governor Palin as a candidate for vice president. However, I am certain that there was not enough positive support written or shown on TV for Governor Palin so that she might have been able to break "through gender barriers," such as the vice presidency of America; and perhaps embarked on her very own path to "a happy ending." I guess people like Rikleen just do not consider Governor Palin enough of a woman to be an acceptable "success story," even though she was in a position to break one of the oldest glass ceilings still in existence. I do not believe that anyone who was alive during the several weeks leading up to the presidential election of 2008 would have disagreed that after August 29, 2008, that Governor Palin was about to enter into her own "gauntlet of scrutiny" by going into some very "unfamiliar territory" of her own.

The sad reality is that the choice of Governor Palin as the VP candidate for the Republican Party was evidence that the mainstream media only takes the time to promote those that meet their criteria: male or female. And sadly, if you do not meet with their approval, they will stop at nothing to make you regret the day you entered the political arena. What happened to the media reporting the news and then letting people make up their own mind? When did the business of controlling outcomes become the media's modus operandi?

To further illustrate how it helps to have the "right stripes" to receive preferential treatment from the media, I would like to explore the words of Ms. Couric herself; spoken just a couple of months prior to anyone in the lower forty-eight ever hearing the name Sarah Palin. At a luncheon in her honor in June 2008, Katie Couric said this: "However you feel about her politics, I feel that Senator [Hillary] Clinton received some of the most unfair, hostile coverage I've ever seen."[47] No problem; that is a fair enough statement. But it does not appear that Ms. Couric made the same effort to defend any of the "unfair" treatment that she actually displayed toward Governor Palin at a time when she could have taken the opportunity to promote the cause of another woman to such a large audience ... well, use your imagination, we are talking CBS. So where were the words of encouragement for Governor Palin? Couric took the time to express concern for a lack of fairness (perceived or real) for Hillary Clinton, but failed to do the same for Governor Palin. Evidently, not all women deserve equal treatment from Couric.

It is extraordinary that Ms. Couric would be so adamant in her belief that there was a supposed lack of fairness and greater hostility shown to Mrs. Clinton, yet somehow not be bothered by a lack of fairness to Governor Palin. Ms. Couric should have the courage to speak out against unfair and hostile treatment of all women, since she happens to have a microphone attached to her on a daily basis. Perhaps Ms. Couric should take a look at the transcripts of Charlie Gibson's interview of Governor Palin. If she were to *view* the tape of that interview with her "fairness" glasses on, I am certain that it would not take her long to recognize the condescension in the manner and tone of Gibson's voice. Couric should be outraged at the way Gibson acted! Here is a small sampling of how Gibson treated Governor Palin:

> GIBSON: "Can you look the country in the eye and say 'I have the experience and I have the ability to be not just vice president, but perhaps president of the United States of America?'
>
> PALIN: I do, Charlie, and on January twentieth, when John McCain and I are sworn in, if we are so privileged to be elected to serve this country, we'll be ready. I'm ready.
>
> GIBSON: And you didn't say to yourself, 'Am I experienced enough? Am I ready? Do I know enough about international affairs? Do I—will I feel comfortable enough on the national stage to do this?'
>
> PALIN: I didn't hesitate, no.
>
> GIBSON: Didn't that take some hubris?"[48]

I am not sure that Charlie Gibson could have been more arrogant. Why does Katie Couric feel any different about Charlie Gibson's interview of Governor Palin than she does about her belief that Mrs. Clinton was treated in a hostile or unfair manner, even now? I suppose since Mrs. Clinton had so much more experience as first lady and as junior senator, which supremely qualified her to be a presidential candidate over someone like Sarah Palin, and that's why she did not deserve to be treated in an unfair manner.

Well, Couric should have been critical of her fellow anchor for his attempts to play "gotcha" journalism with the governor if she were so concerned about the way women are treated. It was painfully obvious to anyone with a shred of decency that Gibson's motive for the interview was not to ascertain the governor's position on the issues, but rather to be absolutely shameful and try to embarrass her.

Why should the media care about the political party affiliation of people that they interview? I have always believed that the media have the responsibility to act as a conduit between the interviewee and the people, to be accurate and fair, especially when it comes to politics. In other words, their mission should only focus on asking pertinent questions and allowing the individual to reply so that the people can then make up their own minds based upon the answers to the questions. I am not saying that tough questions should not be asked of someone seeking to run for political office. I am simply making the point that what is good for one candidate should also be good for another, regardless of party affiliation.

What is unfair or hostile treatment of a liberal candidate ought to apply to a conservative candidate as well. Oftentimes, it seems that those in the national media have an agenda that is in complete contrast to objectivity; even though neutrality is supposed be the motive. Too many media news people spend an inordinate amount of time pushing their personal agenda, and usually make no attempt, or a very poor attempt, at hiding their personal feelings. After all, when you think about it, the people responsible for reporting the news are at the apex of service-related industries and they have the ability to influence the rest of us by the way they report. The people who sit at the anchor's desk ought to be motivated to give us accurate information, unpolluted by personal agendas or opinions. A word to the media: many of us are fully aware and understand your agenda regarding the disdain with which you treat those that do not fit within your politically acceptable mold. Observant people throughout the country acknowledge that many in the mainstream press have not done a very good job hiding their true natures.

Here is another example of someone who also meant well trying to analyze CBS's hiring of Katie Couric. Donna Brazile, former campaign manager for Al Gore during his run for the White House, had this to say: "As in the world of politics, men dominate the dissemination of news. Perhaps that's why I am particularly excited to see Katie Couric at the anchor's desk for the CBS Evening News."[49] I have not paid particular attention to what Ms. Brazile has written about Governor Palin's missed opportunity of blowing through the proverbial glass ceiling. Perhaps she has written much about the governor and I have been irresponsible in my acknowledgment of that fact. If that is the case, I stand corrected.

Since men seem to dominate the world so much, one might think that a woman would do everything and anything in her power to promote any other woman. Some people often put themselves in a corner when their focus is dedicated to things like gender or skin tone. If proponents for the advancement of women are primarily concerned with the progress of women, then the yearning for any other woman who is in a position to be a pioneer in moving forward opportunities for women must be willing to do all within her power to aid in the advancement of a woman—thus extending the possibilities and hopes for all women to be treated equally. In many instances, it seems that the reason women look for validation is due to the fact that they have been severely disrespected in society for their contribution to home, family, community and business. I believe males could do a better job honoring women by showing them the respect that they deserve, recognizing the many contributions they make in our lives, and treating them as equals in business and in society in general.

I think we all recognize the kind of society we have evolved into because of too much emphasis on promoting gender, race, attractiveness, athleticism, IQ, or whatever. It seems that the unintended consequences of such behavior invariably lead to the promotion of a particular someone at the peril of somebody else. In our effort to "establish a more perfect union," we need to be careful about how we divide and categorize people. There are deliberate measures by some in our society to promote a particular class of people over another; this is counterproductive regardless of how noble the intent may be. In an effort to obtain "equality," it is a dangerously slippery slope to promote class distinction for the sole purpose of promoting one human being an unequal advantage over another. No matter how you slice it, the ultimate outcome of promoting one class of people over another results in the potential for other classes feeling the sting of inequality.

SOCIAL OBSERVATIONS

The Declaration of Independence provides for the "pursuit of happiness" even though that right did not always exist for many who have lived in the country in our relatively short history. Please do not equate something like the abolition of slavery with the entitlement mentality that currently exists in our country. Entitlement was born out of the notion that government eventually took upon itself to provide for those they considered disadvantaged or who had been wronged; those that it now considers incapable of pursuing happiness on their own. And unfortunately, many people have been duped into believing that it is the responsibility of government to provide basic necessities of life which they mistakenly believe they somehow deserve because of citizenship.

It was absolutely necessary for the government to be involved in such issues as the abolition of slavery, women's suffrage, and the Civil Rights movement of the mid-twentieth century, for instance. These travesties of social injustice often resulted in the sacrifice of the lives of many people prematurely, thus negating opportunities to pursue happiness to the fullest extent possible. The involvement of good people in government and communities throughout the country was critical so that unjustified treatment of minority classes could be rectified on a national level. Equal protection under the law in the United States today is not only recognized here, but is accepted around the world as well. However, such protections should not be confused with or on parallel to an entitlement attitude.

The 1960s was without doubt a time in which "we the people" behaved horribly with respect to allowing all people to engage in the "pursuit of happiness." However, by the 1970s most communities in America had been liberated of government sponsored discrimination; although the fact remains that we still do not yet live in a colorblind or gender-blind society. Last I checked, both "black" and "white" are colors, but there are also lots of other shades in between that do not often get the same attention. So until we can look beyond superficial characterizations, we will not achieve the kind of unity promoted by the Declaration of Independence. By the way, I do not consider "gender neutrality" to be a superficial characterization because God does not make mistakes. He made us male or female and whatever skin tone we're born with. The mere fact that my skin tone is lighter than someone else's, or that my anatomy is different, does not mean that I cannot be represented in government or business, or whatever, by one whose skin tone is a few shades darker than mine, or whose anatomy does not quite resemble my own.

As a people, we must progress beyond the insignificance of skin color. I believe that skin color and gender mean nothing when it comes to what we have the potential to do. Inherent in my willingness to represent any other person, there must be incorporated the ability to see beyond inconsequential differences. It is not practical in twenty-first century America that a person can only be represented by someone who has the same skin color or similar physical characteristics. I do not care how dark or light the color of someone's skin happens to be or whether they are male or female; they can still represent my interests as a human being. All people deserve to be treated with equal dignity.

I want to illustrate another comment by Donna Brazile, who had this to say about Katie Couric's promotion to anchor at CBS: "Since the announcement, women's groups and leaders have heralded the significance of Couric's ascension. My hero, Gloria Steinem, has been quoted as saying: 'One thing is sure—women and girls will have their first vision of a female network anchor who is an authority on her own. Since we learn by example, there is no telling where that iconic image may lead.' I often wonder how long it will take for women to be truly equal, so that when one of us shatters a glass ceiling, it will not warrant such attention and celebration. What a utopia—or, rather, a meritocracy—we will have achieved when individuals are evaluated and rewarded on accomplishments, without regard for gender and race. We're still far from there, but Couric's hiring brings us one step closer."[50] Anyone familiar with how to speak or write has had plenty of time to defend Governor Palin. Where is the praise for Governor Palin having served as Governor of Alaska? Liberals and women everywhere should consider a woman being elected governor of a state to be just as significant, if not more so, than a woman who is named news anchor of a primetime newscast.

What have we heard from prominent women in our culture with regard to the praise that seems to be reserved for only the "right women" in our society? I am willing to try and uncover the fallacy that is so intertwined in the minds of some in our society with regard to gender and race, for instance. I understand that "white" males have been responsible in the past for perpetuating the twisted ideology designed to keep everyone else down but themselves. But I refuse to feel guilty for the inexcusable behavior of "white" males who have gone before me just because I happen to be a male with light skin tone. Personally, I do not deserve to be judged by that standard. And by the same token, no minority group should embrace the notion that all light-skinned males are somehow still responsible for their lack of upward mobility or achievement. That would be about as smart as an investment firm stating that all publicly traded companies cannot be trusted today because of what happened during the Great Depression.

Repeating Brazile's quote of Gloria Steinem, who said, "One thing is sure—women and girls will have their first vision of a female network anchor … ," I am left to conclude that both Donna Brazile and Gloria Steinem seem to put more importance on the significance of having a female news anchor than on the importance of objective reporting or the significance of a female vice president than of someone serving with honesty and integrity, no matter the gender. It is not a question of which position young girls today might aspire to hold; both positions have relevance even though the job descriptions vary significantly. If it is so essential that "women and girls" have a female anchor to look up to, then how important would it have been to have the first female vice president for women and girls to look up to?

Personally, I am concerned about how women are treated and promoted in our society. I have a wife and daughters and I am confident that they have been, and will still be able to take advantage of opportunities in America to do whatever they choose based upon the amount of effort and work they put into a chosen endeavor. The United States has elected a president who just happens to have skin tone that is a little different than mine. However, that piece of information should not be the determining factor regarding who or what he is. But ultimately, the quality of his performance should be based upon what he does while in office. The color of his skin should not be a factor even though he takes opportunities to address isolated cases like the one in Cambridge at Harvard University. Since when has the office of the President of the United States carried with it the idea that the president must comment about so many unrelated aspects that lie outside the realm of the job description? Most of us just want the president to be Commander in Chief, lead with conviction, and stand up for America!

No one in the twenty-first century should support preferential treatment that acts as a conduit for creating animosity among various groups of people. If preferential treatment based upon race or gender was no big deal in America, then how does one explain the existence of the National Association for the Advancement of Colored People, the National Organization for Women, or the League of United Latin American Citizens? These groups exist for the sole purpose of primarily promoting the race or gender of the people for whom they represent. All three organizations wield political power in America today. I do not believe that anyone is foolish or ignorant enough to not believe that there once was a time that organizations such as these were needed to level the playing field; to give all people a chance to achieve their dreams. Unfortunately, though the Declaration of Independence is a profound document, it took far too long for equality to make the kind of progress desperately needed throughout the early days of our Republic. There are now, however, no restrictions for anyone who decides that the top rung of the ladder is where they want to be. Whether in business, entertainment, sports, or whatever: the sky is truly the limit. By no means am I saying that we have completely eclipsed gender and racial barriers, but by the same token, we have come a long way and that fact should not be forgotten.

With the election of Barack Obama as president, I would say that it is time to take race to the next level. By that I mean that it is time to recognize that "we the people" should begin to acknowledge not only the accomplishments that have already been forged, but even the future accomplishments that all people have the opportunity to achieve irrespective of race, gender, or ethnicity, because living in the United States of America makes it possible. There may be those who conclude that because my skin tone is lighter than most that I am somehow unqualified to make such a statement. I wish I had a different perspective; but just because I do not fit the stereotypical class of one who has been discriminated against does not mean that I have not be discriminated against. I try to live my life each day the way that I have always been taught: "Do unto others as you would have them do unto you." The "golden rule" really is quite simple, and I am confident that no matter the skin color or gender, anyone can observe that rule. So why should I adopt a condition for judging people because of skin color or gender?

Skin color should not enter into the equation when it comes to how we treat each other, and I believe it was God who gave us commandments sufficient to treat each other the right way; though we have all failed to follow such commandments completely, and in every instance suffering has been the result. If you are unsure, talk to anyone who lived during the turbulent racial times of the twentieth century, especially "blacks," and you will have a different perspective on the commandment to "Love thy neighbor." I do not believe that "love" was the motivation for separate but equal. Yet, some narrow-minded people thought that separate worship, restaurants, water fountains, schools, employment—and a host of other things were appropriate ways to enforce the "law," when in reality, the only purpose it served was to further divide "we the people" by emphasizing the most ridiculous superficial reasons for "separate."

Acknowledging bigotry, dealing with it and then moving on is crucial to progress! Anything worthwhile in life may be difficult but not impossible. At this point, I would be willing to settle for our treating one another the way that we ourselves would like to be treated, and changing our attitude so that we can grow beyond the pettiness of what shade our skin happens to be. It is interesting that even though we start out the same way in life; naked and dependent; because of environment, education, experiences, and a host of other factors, we form the philosophy for the way we live most of our lives. Ultimately, where we have been and the things we have done are different and may even be characterized as inequity, especially if you are someone who is over the age of fifty. Nevertheless, anyone blessed to have been born in the United States starts out life with a great shot at succeeding. Even people who have emigrated to the U.S. from other countries have been blessed by what is uniquely American: the Constitution.

At the risk of giving anyone the impression that I believe we're living in a utopian society, rest assured, I am not that gullible. But unfortunately, we seem to be inundated by the thoughts and words of people like Maureen Dowd. I have nothing against Ms. Dowd; I only know her by her words, and as you already know, I believe that words have meaning. In an op-ed piece written on November 9, 2008, Ms. Dowd had this post-Obama victory comment:

> "I saw a white-haired woman down the block from me running out to strike up a conversation with a black UPS delivery guy, asking him how he felt and what this meant to him. I was starting to feel guilty. Every time I passed a *black* patron at a downtown restaurant or a movie or the Kennedy Center, would perfect strangers want me to ask how they were feeling? Or was that condescending and were they sick to death of it? How would I know if I didn't ask them? I heard *my cute black* mailman talking in an excited voice outside my house Friday, so I decided to ask him how he was feeling about everything, the absolute amazement of the first black president... I eagerly swung my front door open and joined

the mailman's conversation. 'Are you talking about the election?' I said brightly. 'How do you feel?' He shot me a look of bemused disdain as he walked away. I suddenly realized, with embarrassment, that he was on his Bluetooth, deep in a personal conversation that had nothing to do with Barack Obama."[51]

How does anyone begin to make sense out of complete and utter nonsense? If a conservative had made even half of the rash statements that Dowd makes in this short quote, oozing with the most sickening condescension, liberals would be pulling their hair out!

Evidently, Dowd won a Pulitzer Prize in 1999 for her "distinguished commentary." I can only imagine how the committee responsible for choosing the person who would receive the Pulitzer that year, actually defined distinguished. Yes, I realize that Dowd's quote is from 2008, which means that Ms. Dowd has had enough practice to come up with something better in the written word than her rambling would indicate. One thing is apparent; Dowd seems to have been intoxicated with the notion of using skin tone as her most important feature when describing some of her fellow human beings. Such an attitude is disgusting and proves that liberals like Dowd seem to be forever motivated by the idea of defining people by the color of their skin.

Frankly, every American should be insulted by the way Ms. Dowd characterized some of her fellow citizens. Her quote is filled with stereotypical nonsense and insensitivity. How are those struggling with racial stereotypes ever going to be able to accept racial equality when people like Dowd write such disturbing material? And even more disturbing, but not surprising, is the fact that her statement cleared the media radar. We have been given a glimpse into the way people like Ms. Dowd seem to think about the need to continue making distinctions based on skin tone. And to be fair, it's not just Dowd who is guilty of such distinctions. Personally, though, I wish she would refrain from writing about her personal idiosyncrasies concerning race; it is not indicative of one who portends that all people are equal; yet apparently has a difficult time describing another human being without making reference to skin color.

Maybe I'm making too big a deal out of this issue, but perhaps everyone like Dowd needs to look at other people as human beings first, and worry less about the color of their skin. We all know people in our society, of any color, whose purpose for living seems to be to continue fanning the flames of distrust among people who don't look like they do. My contention is that as a people, we must move beyond the way someone like Dowd characterizes others by making skin color such a significant fabric.

There is a reason why I put terms like "black" or "white" in quotations throughout this book. When describing a "black" friend to someone else, I do not consider skin tone as relevant; I make the effort to find more significant ways to describe that person. I believe we can do better, especially since most people believe that skin color is not a quality of character. It takes constant effort and creativity, perhaps, to use other methods besides skin color when describing another human being to someone else. Imagine the progress that could be made if we became a more color blind society!

It is clear to me that people like Ms. Dowd are perfectly content to do their part to continue driving a wedge of division further into the heart of America, while at the same time giving the impression that they are genuinely concerned about leaving the divisive stereotypes associated with bigotry behind.

"After 9/11, the White House and Capitol were ever more blockaded, and there seemed to be fewer and fewer bridges across any of our divisions—racial, political, social, and cultural. But now we have the delicious irony that a white president from a patrician family, whose administration was so negligent about America's poor and black citizens, was so incompetent that he helped elect the first black president … It's cool that President-elect Cool has gotten everybody chatting, even if it's awkward small talk. And it's fun, after so many years of unyielding barriers, to feel sentimental."[52]

Do we now have to refer to Obama as "President Cool" since he supposedly has "everybody chatting" about how we are now one big happy family? Dowd seems to be under the impression that it is the Obama administration's responsibility to overcome social issues like helping "America's poor and black citizens." Whatever happened to personal responsibility and the people working together to achieve equality amongst ourselves?

Apparently, Dowd is also a little confused about where she lives and what form of government exists here in America because of her comment about a "patrician family." Though I have not completed former president Bush's genealogy, perhaps he does have noble blood running through his veins; however, that is not going to do him a whole lot of good since we do not live under aristocratic rule here in America. Besides, as a U.S. citizen, I am certain that he would not get too far using the nobility card, though he might enjoy trying. Yet, this did not stop Ms. Dowd from making such an irresponsible comment, giving us a glimpse into what she must be thinking of the intellectual capacity of her readers.

The notion that every negative and challenging event that took place during George W. Bush's presidency is somehow his fault—whether man-made or otherwise—is nothing more than a huge stretch of the imagination. However, various members of the media have gone to great lengths to get people all over the world to believe such lunacy.

Ms. Dowd mentioned that the election of Barack Obama "has gotten everybody chatting, even if it's awkward small talk. And it's fun, after so many years of unyielding barriers, to feel sentimental." It is unfortunately left to the imagination exactly what she meant by her use of the phrase "unyielding barriers."

To be "unyielding" is to not bend; to not be flexible. I do not know of any "barriers" impeding the way to success for any person in America today, even when Bush was in the White House. If one is willing to endure hard work and make the effort to be dedicated to achieve, anyone can realize the kind of success that is possible in America. Just because Ms. Dowd feels "awkward" while talking to someone that does not look, act, dress, or think like her, does not necessarily mean that the rest of us feel the same way.

If I did not know any better, I would think that this type of rhetoric was written by Ms. Dowd during another century; one which was marred by slavery and the most heinous kinds of bigotry and brutality. I believe that this type of language is an elementary attempt at self-expression and a view that is not shared by very many people today. I am not in denial about the fact that we live in a racially diverse culture today, but that does not negate the fact that we all need some very common things to get by in life, in spite of our diversity. There used to be a time, not too many years ago, in which America was referred to as a melting pot. Can any other nation boast that it is a mix of people made up of so many unique cultures joined together by the greatest Constitution known to mankind? Perhaps, but it seems to me that it is time to put an end to attaching labels to humans as "black" or "white." I am annoyed because of the time in which we are now living; that there are still those who perpetuate worn-out ideas of stereotype, regardless of how blatant or subtle they may be.

I believe Dowd's words should be condemned by honest seekers of equality in our society. I am only recommending condemning Ms. Dowd's *words* because she, too, is afforded the right to say and write what she wants, no matter how much I disagree with it. But the practice of characterizing people with color labels must come to an end.

Obviously, there are still some general hang-ups in our country when it comes to race; there is an apparent need that such information be gathered for seemingly scheming plans by those in high places, particularly among liberals. And it would seem that I am not that far from the truth, since the idea of taking over the Census Bureau by the Obama administration and issues over the 2010 census is reality. I guess they want to be able to micro-manage the reporting of such data so that they can then manipulate it to best support their effort to organize on a community-type basis nationally. We will have to wait and see how White House Chief of Staff Rahm Emanuel[53] will handle that one. I am sure the Obama team intends nothing but the best for all people to be the outcome from such a move. It is my belief that any human being, no matter the skin tone or gender, is capable of representing a constituency so long as their desire is to serve the people. I have no problem with such an approach, nor should anyone else since that is how the founders set it up. So long as personal liberties are not violated, why would any of us care about the gender or color of one elected to represent us? A census is supposed to provide the numbers of people in a given area so that adequate representation can take place, not a manufactured count that can be skewed to give an unfair advantage to a select group of people, or provide the government with more information than it needs to know.

Because we live in an entitlement society, I suppose liberals will always feel as if their job is incomplete. Politicians and the media need to address issues faced by all human beings and the challenges that we sometimes face, and there must be an end to the efforts by some to pit one group against another. Everyone needs to be free from government control and media bias so that they can continue to pursue the happiness that's best for them. It is time to end the requirements that insist that we describe each other by color, ethnicity, or race. We live at a time when it is not necessary that representatives in Congress look just like the people they are elected to represent. If we are going to base representation on such unimportant criteria like skin color, then we truly have a long way to go. Such expectations would imply that only a deaf person could represent another deaf person; only a blind person could represent a blind person; only a paralyzed person could represent another paralyzed person; only a blond could represent another blond. That may seem ridiculous, but it is the logical sequence.

In his book, *My Grandfather's Son,* Clarence Thomas makes a very distressing statement when he says that:

> ... in the years following Dr. [Martin Luther] King's assassination, affirmative action (though it wasn't yet called that) had become a fact of life at American colleges and universities, and before long I realized that those blacks who benefited from it were being judged by a double standard. As much as it stung to be told that I'd done well in the seminary despite my race, it was far worse to feel that I was now at Yale because of it. I sought to vanquish the perception that I was somehow inferior to my white classmates by obtaining special permission to carry more than the maximum number of credit hours by taking a rigorous curriculum of courses... How could anyone dare to doubt my abilities if I excelled in such demanding classes? But it was futile for me to suppose that I could escape the stigmatizing effects of racial preference, and I began to fear that it would be used forever after to discount my achievements.[54]

It is shameful that Justice Thomas or any other person, male or female, be faced with the task of enduring such stigma. Why should one whose pigmentation happens to be different than someone else's be made to feel as if he must do something extra, above and beyond what his peers must do, just to be validated? It was wrong in Clarence Thomas's case and it is wrong for anyone today to believe that in order to "vanquish the perception," that he or she must do something more than that which a peer is required to do. The only way to discard preferences based on sex or race is to wholly and completely overhaul attitudes.

Now I completely understand that there were millions of people who voted to elect Barack Obama president on merit and potential alone; so I believe we can safely say that the election of Obama as president has finally put to rest the question of equality in America and the need for racial preferences or quotas. Evidently, someone like Ms. Dowd seems to have been one who voted for Obama based on overwhelming guilt for the atrocities committed by her forefathers; that is assuming she did indeed vote for Obama.

I am neither proud nor ashamed to say that I did not vote for Barack Obama. However, anyone who knows me recognizes that my not voting for him had nothing to do with the shade of his skin. There were myriad reasons I did not vote for him, but none having to do with his skin tone, color, pigmentation, or any other physical characteristic. Conversely, the fact that I voted for McCain also had nothing to do with race. Incidentally, he was nowhere near my first choice.

Perpetuating a negative belief or stereotype about women, race, or ethnicity because it may have been the position of one who preceded us in life does not mean it is worthy to continue. My parents' generation, as well as previous generations, may have been raised during times of great skepticism with respect to interacting with those of a different race or ethnicity. There was also, not that long ago even, great skepticism about the worth of females. For those who doubt, ponder for a moment why it took fifty years after "blacks" received the right to vote for women, of any skin type, to finally gain the same privilege. I am merely stating a fact. Should we be surprised that America has yet to elect a female president or vice president? There are often reports about the continuing disparity with regard to equality of pay for equal work when comparing men with women. Human beings make decisions every day that involve discrimination.

Generally speaking, we are no longer living at a time of such blatant racial inequality and bigotry. Sure, there are still pockets of racial discrimination among both "blacks" and "whites" in America; and it is within these pockets of racial hatred that people just need to get over themselves and learn how to live together. I believe that most people today do not have the kinds of concerns about a person's skin color.

The way to start, for those wondering how to take the next step, is simple. Begin today by seeing all people as human beings, not specific sub-categories of human beings. Make the effort to accept the fact that you are no better than any of the billions of people now walking the planet. Obviously, this will not be easy for some people, because it will require the intellectual honesty needed in order to see character instead of the tendency to see a shade of color.

I accept the notion that there are those who do not believe that racism is dead in America. But as far as I am concerned it is, though I cannot control the opinions and thoughts of others. Even so, the way to move forward is to root out cases of bigotry, condemn them for what they are, and educate people about the fact that we all originate from the same God; we are all His children no matter what shade of skin covers our vertebrate frames. All Americans would do well to observe young people today who have no problem embracing what was once perceived as being off limits or forbidden unless your skin was a certain color. The world in which we now live is so much more open than it once was with regard to race, and that is a good thing. That does not cancel out the fact that there are people living today who have endured racial bigotry. But just as with any physical wound that eventually heals; so to can the mental and emotional scars of bigotry heal with time when approached with the right attitude.

I realize that there are those living today who have witnessed the hate and injustice of bigots in our society long since the abolishment of slavery. I do not know why it took over 100 years after emancipation for "blacks" to gain equal access to all that white males had a complete right to since the days of our founding; I only know that it is a huge blemish on America's history that full equality was not extended to all citizens regardless of race or gender at the time of the establishment of our nation. We need to face the fact that hatred and bigotry lie at the root of most of the injustice perpetrated against those in our society who look different. Sadly, we may have to wait until all the old, backward thinkers leave the planet before we can finally look at racism and sexism from the rearview mirror.

We may *never* live in a society where greater harmony will prevail over disunity, but it does not mean that we stop working toward it. It is possible to move beyond a perpetual discussion about all the differences that exists among us and look instead for what we have in common. All of us desire to be understood, to have food, water, acceptance, money, etc. No one could possibly believe the madness that water somehow provides greater benefit to women than it does for men; or that "whites" need to be any less understood than "blacks." Nor is the value of a dollar dependent on whom the giver or the receiver happens to be. If these scenarios seem absurd, then I am probably making my point. From my perspective, it is just as absurd to devote constructive time to endless debate about the need to give preferential treatment to a particular class of people. Is there any reason for a politician, a member of the media, or any other person to treat one group of people any different than another? No amount of discrimination or racism today will make up for past discriminatory behavior.

Oftentimes the media give the impression that they would rather fan the flames of division or disagreement than lead the cause to extinguish them; the most recent general election is proof of that. We seem to always get exposed to reports on how women, "blacks," or Hispanics voted; I fail to see the significance for such polling. Why do those in the media often exploit polling data for their own scheming designs? It seems to be counter to forming "a more perfect union" if we have some in our society that do whatever they can to make sure that the rest of us remember that we all belong to our "separate but equal" enclaves. And polling at election time or any other does just that. I remember the huge struggle our country faced trying to eliminate the failed social experiment of "separate but equal."

I am not a polling expert, nor do I pretend to understand the science regarding the nature of polls. I realize that it is difficult to obtain quality, truthful information, and then disseminate that information in a meaningful unbiased way. Furthermore, who really cares how other people vote? If there are those who are so adamant about conducting polls, why not simply conduct a poll on what *people* think? And if there needs to be some distinction, break it down by male and female only. Who needs to know how women or any other demographic votes? And if you tell me jobs depend on it that simply lends credence to my argument. Besides, I thought voting was supposed to be a personal and private matter.

Some people are very much inclined to create divisions by race, color, creed, religion, rich and poor, and on and on because that often seems to be the way some people in government and social fields want it, and polling data only validates their vision of "separate but equal." We have been conditioned in so many ways. But what about the not-so-popular divisions like short, fat, skinny, stupid, homely, or idiotic; just to name a few? All of these divisions and many more deal primarily in the superficial, not the substantive.

It is not just the major political parties and the media that are guilty of manipulating polling data or making judgments based on anything less than substance; employers do it as well. If people are going to get so upset about our government performing ethnic or racial profiling, then we had better be equally upset when nearly all modeling agencies and other employers concerned about image engage in profiling on a daily basis. And may I be so bold as to say that such profiling can be just as damaging to an individual. For instance, how dare the makers of *Speedo* give anyone over a certain body weight the impression that they are not eligible to model the latest fashion in swimwear; a 400 pound man should be able to model the latest *Speedo* fashion if that is his passion and he works hard enough to make it. Perhaps the makers of *Speedo* are just trying to make a profit by selling their product by using proven marketing techniques. Sorry Mr. 400 hundred pounder, find something else to do for a living. Seriously though, why is it not okay to profile in order to protect American citizens, but perfectly acceptable to do so and stunt the growth of one who may not fit the perfect "profile" to model swimwear?

Many in our society tend to focus on appeasement, pacification, and pandering instead of really talking about issues with progression as the objective. And I mean real progression, not the perceived progressiveness of a political movement whose philosophy is anything but progressive. For instance, I have never figured out how ending the life of an unborn child is synonymous with progress; it seems more barbaric than progress. How can we consider it progressive for a woman to have the right to choose whether another human being is allowed to experience mortality? All things being equal, a committed father should have his "right to choose" not to abort. Again, all things being equal, it seems that males should have just as much a right to fatherhood under the right circumstances. I believe that women should choose to give birth and that men should choose to be responsible and commit to the relationship. One of the few things I learned in high school science class was that it takes sperm from a male getting together with an egg from a female to create a fetus and put it on the fast track to becoming a citizen. In either case, it seems that in a multitude of instances the decision to abort or give birth to a child is contingent upon the choice to have sexual intercourse; which I have to assume is a decision most people view themselves as being "pro choice."

Progressiveness should mean that we are willing to focus on the future, without forgetting sound morals and principles from the past. Making a choice based upon what is expedient is usually not a good thing, though it is often referred to as progressive. Sometimes it is *not* about finding common ground, because that may mean a compromise of principles, which I view as unacceptable just for the sake of finding common ground. I believe there is still something called right and wrong. As far as political party, it is about time that we put an end to the presumptuous nature of cookie-cutting based on race or gender. I think it is completely absurd that all rich "white" guys are presumed to be members of the Republican Party and that all urban "blacks" are supposed to be part of the Democratic Party. These norms do nothing to change attitudes and beliefs about race or ethnicity because of the conditioning that many have experienced and embraced. But I believe real education and enlightenment can and must be achieved, even if it means accepting outcomes that fly in the face of conventional wisdom.

I am not aware of anything that a citizen of the United States is prohibited from doing within the bounds of the law today, irrespective of race or gender. Some may contend, and rightfully so that in order to become president or vice president of the United States, it would probably help if you were not a woman, given the outcome of every single election since George Washington. However, I believe that there are women that could care less if we ever have a female president, or "blacks" that could care less if we have a "black" president. Most of us want to be confident that limitless possibilities are available to us no matter what since most of us will never be president of the United States.

Hopefully, the election of Barack Obama will lead to the beginning of the end of bigotry in America; seems as good a place to begin as any other. I suppose it is only a matter of time before we have a female president, thus signaling the release of our country from the grips of gender conflicts. If so-called minorities have ascended to the tops of the ladder, then opportunities certainly abound for everyone. It is about time that we accept the fact that discrimination is wrong on every level, no matter how it's packaged. The bottom line is that if it is wrong for "blacks" and women to be discriminated against, then it is wrong for any person to be so treated regardless of race, creed, color, ethnicity, physical appearance or mental capacity.

LIPS CAN STOP VERY LITTLE FOR GOOD OR ILL

Why is it that what we see politicians do often seems to be drastically different than what we may have heard them say? Surely, they are not just concerned about impressing their listeners with no intention of following through on promises they have made. I might add that we are not talking a mere slip of the tongue, but a deliberate attempt to promise what they must surely know they cannot possibly deliver. Why do we allow these people to get away with saying one thing during the course of a campaign and then permit them to forget that they made such comments? Furthermore, why do we allow such behavior to continue after the perpetrator has been sworn in? I would think that most people consider such behavior a blatant attempt to manipulate the electorate, at best; and flat-out lying, worst case scenario. But in today's "feel good" politics, the people seem to be getting what they vote for: style over substance. I suppose our founding documents make provisions for that as well. Unfortunately, in politics there are seldom ever consequences paid, especially if you have the right kind of charisma and enough of the people like you.

We need to take a look at a politician who essentially epitomized perfection in the art of making people believe one thing and then reneging on pretended beliefs. During the most recent presidential campaign, to be fair, both Obama and McCain said and did things throughout the course of the campaign that were frankly unbelievable. Like Obama repeating over and over how he was going to have the debate about health care reform on

CSPAN. Or like McCain suspending his campaign during the "financial crises" to return to Washington, as if anything else happening in the Senate prior to that and during the course of the campaign was not that important. The people have come to accept this as typical campaign politics.

Everyone knows that Obama was the candidate that primarily ran his campaign on themes of "change," "yes, we can," and "transparency." I have no problem at all with such noble premises for a campaign. I will admit, it seemed to work really well; so congratulations to the person or persons who came up with the idea. However, it was interesting to see the kind of "change" we would be subject to when Obama took office. We even had a glimpse of the kind of change Obama had been talking about throughout the campaign in the weeks leading up to the inauguration. Not only do I not approve of his "change" since he's been in the White House, but we should have been wise to his desire to make the bureaucracy even more controlling when he created the "office of the president-elect," and even had a logo created so it could be fastened to the podium whenever he spoke. I'm not sure what part of the Constitution allows for such action. It was not enough for him to be patient and wait until after his inauguration to have the real logo and official Seal of the President of the United States located on nearly every lectern he speaks from.

Unfortunately, it seems that his idea of "change" and mine do not exactly square; I think there are a lot of people who probably feel the same way. It is interesting that when it came time for Obama to make his cabinet appointments, that there were a whole lot of people who had ties to the Clinton presidency, which seemed like quite a stretch for one who claimed to be the candidate for "change." Perhaps Obama was simply admitting that he did not have the executive experience, or the right people advising him on all matters presidential. I suppose the one big "change" was the fact that Mr. Obama seemed to have a knack for appointing people to cabinet positions who tried to get out of paying their fair share of taxes.

It is interesting to note Bush's philosophy regarding country's that did not cooperate with the US in our effort to root out terrorism, when he said that: "You're either with us or against us in the fight against terror."[55] Oh, how he was ridiculed for being too abrasive and unilateral. But when Obama made a similarly unilateral comment relative to closing tax loopholes in America, it did not seem to ruffle any feathers or draw a whole lot of criticism by those guilty of doing the same thing to Bush. Mr. Obama said that: "If financial institutions won't cooperate with us, we will assume that they are sheltering money in tax havens and act accordingly."[56] This statement sounds a bit on the one-sided front as far as I'm concerned, and I do not think it is the kind of "change" that typical Americans expected from the *Commander in Change*. If this is the kind of thing he is talking about; what is it that he has yet to say that may be dramatically more radical? And to top it off, the Bush comment concerning terrorism seems to be much more consequential for ill as opposed to people looking to slip one past the government by exploiting loopholes in the tax code.

Yes, the Commander in Chief sometimes has to make decisions without the comfort or luxury of multilateral decisiveness; whereas Obama seemed to waste no time going after American citizens who use perfectly legal loopholes to minimize their tax liabilities. I know we are talking apples and oranges because it is difficult to compare terrorism to the tax code, though the tax code itself could be considered a form of economic terrorism to everyone who is subjected to it. Perhaps it is time for President Obama to examine and scrutinize the tax code in America with the same intensity that Bush used in going after the terrorists.

Speaking of which, here is another tidbit from Bush in his accurate assessment of the Taliban, who, "try and impose their radical views through threats … We see the same intolerance of dissent, the same mad global ambitions, the same brutal determination to control every life and all of life."[57] If I did not know better, I would have thought that Bush was forecasting the efforts of a future administration to control the lives of everyday Americans, particularly those not in agreement with every decision made.

Please pay attention to the direction the facts seem to be pointing with the intention of the Obama administration to go after people here, and how similar it is to Bush's comments about going after the Taliban: To "control every life and all of life" by trying to "impose their radical views through threats … " and by exhibiting their potential for "intolerance of dissent," as indicated in his comments to go after financial institutions who "won't cooperate with us." Mr. Obama himself said that, "we will assume that they are sheltering money in tax havens and act accordingly." It is disturbing for the president of the United States to make such comments because it gives the appearance that he is more interested in going after Americans who use legitimate loopholes to minimize their tax burden. But in both instances, taxes and the Taliban, it will require more than just tough talk to get the job done.

Believe it or not, a lot of people are concerned about the bottom line, among other things, and the American people should not be treated like the enemy. If the president wants to make a name for himself and secure the adulation of informed people—the kind that many in the country exhibited for him during the campaign due to sheer ignorance—then he must be the kind of president that is friendly to the people who provide the jobs for the 95% of tax payers he supposedly claims to be looking out for, and for whom he promised would not see their taxes increase "one dime."

As I have previously stated, I did not vote for Mr. Obama; however, I have no ill will toward the man; he is my president as much as anyone else's. Nevertheless, like Rush Limbaugh, I cannot hope for his success when it comes to the possibility of his philosophy or policies becoming the law of the land. As of this moment, it remains to be seen what the full impact of the second "stimulus" package will ultimately have on our economy. One thing we know for sure, it has exponentially increased the size and scope of the government like never before. We heard over and over during the campaign that 95% of Americans were going to get a tax cut when Mr. Obama became president; and that he would only raise taxes on people making over $250,000 a year, though that figure was in a constant state of fluctuation since the first utterance of 95%.

It seems to be well known that when the government cuts taxes, revenues to the federal government typically increase because fewer people are less concerned with finding the loopholes that minimize the tax burden. Law abiding citizens don't mind paying their fair share of taxes if the tax rate is actually fair. So Mr. Obama should make the Bush tax cuts, set to expire in 2010, permanent; because not extending those tax cuts is equivalent to a tax increase, likely on many in the 95% crowd that Obama promised would not see their taxes raised. Any other talk of tax increases, no matter the approach, will do exactly what Obama has said would not happen—increase taxes on those making less than 250k per year.

Behavior exhibited by Mr. Obama during the campaign of 2008 is not uncommon for those seeking power from a political office. Both democrats and republicans do the same thing to one degree or another; and by no means is such behavior restricted to presidential campaigns. Seeking power in the government seems to be pathological among many people, who use the ballot box to attempt to validate themselves; which power often then becomes the hallmark of those whose purpose is supposed to be centered on me and you.

The question seems to be rather simple: What are we going to do with people who are so over-zealous during the course of a campaign that they will say just about anything to get elected; and who realize that the media will not hold them to account, especially if that upper-case (D) happens to follow their name?

How about if every candidate elected to public office is honorable and decent, the person we expect, who explains to the people in clear and unmistakable terms what he will or will not do for the people, should he be fortunate enough to receive the blessing of the people. I realize that it stands to reason that the more ambiguous a candidate and his positions, the more he hopes that "we the people" will not bother to try and understand or grasp the complex nuances of government jargon. And I guess it then becomes even easier to make the supposedly complex look even more so when those same people get elected; sort of like being easier to ask for forgiveness than to ask for permission. I am not a lawyer, but many candidates for public office happen to be; I'm not sure how beneficial that is to the rest of us.

There would certainly be a lot more trees that could be saved with fewer lawyers in office, and even fewer advising them; legislation would naturally be shortened to reflect the kind of language typically spoken by regular folks, since lawyers tend to say in three pages what the rest of us can say in a paragraph. And how dare any lawyer-member of Congress condescend beneath dignity to tell the American people that legislation must consist of confusing legal language in order to be considered legitimate!

The American people should be disturbed to know how many hundreds of tree parts were wasted on the Economic Stimulus package and health reform legislation that no one in Congress bothered to even read, not that they would have had the time or the inclination to do so before casting their vote one way or the other. Remember, we were told that time was of the essence and that a bill had to be signed by the president to prevent the most horrible economic crises since the Great Depression from getting even worse. By the way, I wonder how that great piece of legislation is working out for everyone. I do not believe the president has ensured that everyone who wants to work actually has a job, because last I checked, we still have unemployment—like we always will. And it will always be worse than what politicians actually say it is, because it is impossible to account for everyone who has been out of work long term.

And with respect to health care legislation, the American people have been subjected to the most coercive language uttered by politicians in recent memory. Everyone who supports the government being involved in some kind of health care reform from the president on down has been guilty of trying to scare the people into accepting their version of reform so that more people won't needlessly lose their lives. Yet none of these people seem to enjoy addressing the issue that there are thousands of pages that comprise the most aggressive takeover of any private sector industry in recent memory. Most Americans would be satisfied with legislation that is straightforward and to the point. And I dare say that most informed Americans are not satisfied with the passage of health care reform.

If you take the time to research and actually read a particular bill, you will be amazed to see hundreds of pages of needless repetition and references to lots of other federal laws, most of which make absolutely no sense. Now if you are trying to teach a dog how to sit or beg, or you are teaching a toddler how to walk, or drink out of something other than a sippy cup, then repetition is a good thing. However, we do not need it in the form of legislation to the extent that we now have it, especially when it sends you on a wild goose chase just to be able to figure out the meaning of a reference to another law!

If you are still not convinced by my lamenting over lengthy legislation, take some time on a weekend when you are mysteriously bored out of your head and try reading the stimulus bill or any version of health care reform that Congress has passed or is reconsidering; but don't say I didn't warn you. Realistically, most of us will never take the time to read something like that; but if we did, it would more than likely compel us to vote against anyone who had anything to do with its creation. Congress seems to have a love affair when it comes to passing legislation on totally meaningless nonsense, which for all the legal minds out there, do not infer that there is such a thing as meaningful nonsense. Once again, most of us would be content to have Congress pass legislation that makes sense to the American people, and that does not rival a half dozen good novels in length. Perhaps it is time to amend the Constitution to ban anyone who is a lawyer from running for office.

For as long as I can remember, most candidates who hope to have an opportunity of working on the kind of lengthy legislation we have just discussed spend far too much time criticizing their opponent and digging for dirt in hopes of getting into office to do the very thing I have just complained about. Every election cycle we hear the same old routine about how the campaigning style is going to be different; more tranquil and harmless. But after the elections we wonder what happened to all the good intentions. I believe that the majority of people want to be able to hear the candidate directly articulate the issues, specifically what they intend to do to preserve and defend the Constitution upon being elected. When a candidate is elected, but fails to follow through on every campaign promise, that person no longer deserves to be re-elected because we cannot trust what has come out of their mouth.

Regardless of political party, every politician is obligated to the people to follow through on what they promise; although when a liberal fails to adhere to their proposed promises, the consequences are usually better for the rest of us, but accountability is no less important. Politicians like to talk about what they think makes people feel good; and "feel good" politics is usually not a good thing, regardless of the political party.

What is a political discussion about "feel good" politics without the mention of the king of "feel good," William Jefferson Clinton? I am fascinated by Mr. Clinton's efforts to rewrite the history of his presidency. It is one thing to talk about what your administration accomplished while you were in office, but it is something altogether different when you continue to pontificate about it years after leaving office; and it seems to be a favorite pastime of Mr. Clinton's, because he has done a good bit of it since leaving the presidency. To illustrate this point, I want to explore a speech given by the former president at Georgetown University in 2006, about *Securing the Common Good*. Please remember, this is just one speech!

GOVERNMENT BY LIBERALS, FOR LIBERALS

It is not unusual for former presidents to be in the public domain upon leaving office. And often, former presidents do some of their most important work after leaving office, including Clinton. He has done some great work with his foundation as well as helping to alleviate suffering by those who have experienced the wrath of natures furry. Notwithstanding, it seems that Mr. Clinton leads the pack when it comes to getting his mug on the air upon leaving the White House. Looking back over the last few decades, there has probably not been a former president more gleeful to be in front of the camera than Bill Clinton. Granted, the evolution of the 24/7 media culture has made that more of a reality than perhaps it might have otherwise been; and it doesn't hurt that Clinton is a media darling with potentially many more years to be seen by the rest of us. Imagine for a moment if Johnson or Nixon would have been in the limelight after their presidency as much as Clinton has been. Of course, Carter has had his moments in the public eye, mostly because he probably has such overwhelming guilt because of one of the most unsuccessful administrations in the last 100 years! Obviously, in Nixon's case, he most likely had no desire to have a camera anywhere near his face; and fortunately for him, the media was only too willing to accommodate. What about Ford, Reagan, or George H.W. Bush? Aside from humanitarian efforts and libraries, these former presidents were (have been) fairly content to fade away into somewhat obscure private life;

and it is probably safe to assume that George W. Bush will follow suit. I cannot imagine a stampede of media elites making their way to Crawford, Texas, to get the latest on W's opinions.

> Let's start with this from Clinton: "The empowerment zones, the enterprise communities, all the urban development initiatives, the welfare reform initiatives ... When we passed the budget in 1993, it was passed by one vote in a strict party line vote—one vote in both houses. It raised taxes on upper-income people, raised the gas tax 4.3 percent as I remember, and cut taxes on lower income working families. Fifteen times as many people got a tax cut as a tax increase. We doubled the Earned Income Tax Credit. That alone took over two million children out of poverty. When we raised the minimum wage, it lifted the earnings of ten million people. And I tried to do it twice, and we haven't done it since. We provided more health care options for low-income families. We had the biggest expansion in health care coverage since Medicaid in the sixties with the Children's Health Insurance Program. We had the biggest increase in college aid since the G.I. Bill at the end of World War II. Ten million more people were getting college assistance through tax credits or Pell grants or work-study programs than when we started. Average hourly wages actually went up in my second term ... The number of people without health insurance went down. I could keep you here all day talking about other statistics ... "[58]

I bet he could, and thankfully I was not there to listen to the whole thing. Apparently, I missed out on how he singlehandedly alleviated all suffering in the 1990s; we were living in Utopia during his years in office and I did not even realize it. After a presidency that included all of that and so much more, how could we possibly accept the fact that there are economically downtrodden citizens that exist among us today? If it is possible to identify the most blatant falsehood about the previous quote, perhaps it is that the former Commander in Chief stated that 2 million children were taken out of poverty by his doubling the

Earned Income Tax Credit (EITC). I do not recall what the amount of the EITC happened to be at any time during the Clinton years, but for the sake of argument, let's assume that the EITC was $3,000 (multiplied by the number of qualifying dependents); he wants us to believe that a few thousand dollars in the form of a tax credit actually took 2 million children out of poverty? This is absurd. How long would it have taken for someone of little means to blow through a few thousand bucks?

Judging by the economic turmoil that still exists for many Americans, things have not exactly improved for the economically depressed because of EITC payments received during the Clinton years. And incidentally, EITC given during the Bush years seems to have had identical results; the difference is that Bush is not out stumping about how his tax credits took "2 million children off the poverty roles." Most likely, Obama will be content to run with the same Clinton torch; but will most likely compound the situation by his ideologically driven redistribution tactics.

Maybe Clinton meant to say that it took 2 million children in a severe state of poverty and put them in a somewhat better position of poverty; if that is the case then perhaps he was right. But I am inclined to believe that it is complete and utter gibberish that just because a family received a check during the Clinton years for a few thousand dollars, that suddenly they're off the poverty rolls. Perhaps the most disappointing aspect of Clinton's comments are that he seems to honestly believe what he says; and virtually no one in the media is willing to question the validity of his statements. Perhaps many are content to regard him as the old uncle in his rocking chair, regurgitating all sorts of folklore tales about his past that no one bothers to question, nor do they care. But like the story telling uncle, we tend to feel sorry for a former president who resorts to fables when describing parts of his administration. As much as Mr. Clinton probably believes that he gets hammered by the media;

he should, perhaps, get in touch with the forty-third president, so as to squash any such notions.

The really sad piece of information is that it does not seem to matter what liberals say, because they are judged for how they deliver the message, and by the way it makes people feel, not by whether it is true or not. The really good ones can convince their listeners to believe practically anything that comes out of their mouth. As a matter of fact, they usually convince them that what they are saying is factual since they are rarely challenged anyway. Even though someone like Bush came across as genuine, it did not seem to matter for many in the mainstream media because he was just too folksy and simplistic for modern-day media elitism to endure.

We ought to be accustomed to the type of hair-splitting rhetoric from Clinton after all these years; honestly, half of the time I want to believe him myself when he says things like: "The problem with ideology is, if you've got an ideology, you've already got your mind made up. You know all the answers and that makes evidence irrelevant and argument a waste of time, so you tend to govern by assertion and attack. The problem with that is, that discourages thinking and gives you bad results."[59] I wonder who he had in mind when he made this statement, because it sounds a lot like his fellow democrat, Barack Obama. How often did Obama go on the "attack" concerning health care reform?

The implication of Clinton's "ideology" remark smacks at the notion that the former president was actually referring to people in the *other* party, especially his reference to governing by "assertion and attack." Heaven knows that democrats embrace very little on the ideology home front, so therefore, could not possibly be guilty of having their minds made up about a particular idea! So what was the objective of Clinton's argument relative to the public good? Clinton's ideology remark seems to erode the premise of the former president's argument because democrats and republicans traditionally have espoused divergent ideological philosophies, but they exist nonetheless. Perhaps he was trying to say that *his* political philosophy cannot be defined ideologically; and if he cannot define it, then who? But then again, it is possible that it may have been one of those situations similar to the old—depends on what the "definition of *is*, is."

In all sincerity, I find it amusing that anyone would actually believe this man, least of all, himself! He goes on to say that "I think it's important to point out that if you're an ideologue, denial is an essential part of your political being—whichever side. If you're an ideologue, you've got your mind made up, so when an inconvenient fact pops up, you have to be in denial."[60] So Mr. Clinton wants us to believe that as an ideologue, "denial is an essential part of your political being—whichever side." I guess we are to surmise that Bill Clinton is not an ideologue or that he has just not committed to one side or the other.

I suppose Clinton is doing his best to tell us that he is not an ideologue. However, does that mean that he is not able to make up his mind when it comes to making principled decisions regardless of the consequences? Of course, only conservatives can be ridiculed for failing to live up to their principles since liberals claim exemption status when it comes to being principled.

In the arena of ideas, there must continue to be healthy debate, whether someone thinks you're an ideologue or not. I wonder if the former president considers that anyone who ever championed the cause of equal rights for "blacks" to have been or to be an ideologue. Where would we be today if the ideology of equality had not been recognized or accepted in America so that all people could ultimately be blessed by our unique founding documents?

Before jumping to conclusions about what I may or may not think about Bill Clinton's ideology; I am not saying that he was in favor of denying civil rights to "blacks." But how do we justify his comments about what he thinks an ideologue is without it being in conflict with the ideological pursuit of equal rights for blacks? Is he saying that those who had their minds made up about the need for equal rights were somehow in "denial?" Words mean things.

In his own words Mr. Clinton seems to believe that when you embrace a particular ideology, you must also accept that "denial is an essential part of your political being." It is sometimes difficult to determine if he actually believes his own rhetoric or if he is just speaking from the political expediency playbook. I do know that when the former president gets behind a microphone, he seems to think he can say whatever he wants to say without regard to facts or consequences. I wish Mr. Clinton would be more precise and identify a particular ideology that he does adhere to so that we could then assess his capacity to deny an important part of his "political being." I actually appreciate the ideology espoused by all those that fought for equal rights in our country, and who seek for equality in countries across the earth.

What were the body of ideas reflecting the social needs and aspirations of "blacks" in the mid-twentieth century in the United States? How about the need for equal treatment under the law; the right to be able to walk through the front door of any restaurant to enjoy a meal; the right to use any public restroom; the right to drink out of any water fountain; the right to ride public transportation and sit in any seat; essentially, the right to be given access to the freedom that anyone else in society enjoyed. And even though it took entirely too long for all citizens in the U.S. to receive equal treatment, God be thanked for all those willing to speak up and reject the nonsense coming through the lips of bigots.

I do not believe Mr. Clinton has ever been a proponent for unequal treatment of "blacks." On the contrary, it seems as though he has been a staunch advocate of the equal treatment of all people, even though his liberal policies have done little to assist people in recognizing their true potential to live beyond anything the government can do for them. Bill Clinton seems to think that he can have something mean one thing to one group and something else to another group. Granted, there have been ideas embraced by ideologues in the past like Adolf Hitler and Joseph Stalin that have been harmful to people on a grand scale. But if Mr. Clinton is going to assert his definition of an ideologue because it suits him, and then expect the rest of us to accept it as gospel, that is something I cannot do. It would appear as though Clinton has unwittingly put himself at the top of the list according to his definition of an ideologue. I cannot imagine that that was his intention.

There seems to be a dilemma for liberals who desire to paint history the way they see it, irrespective of the facts. They like to describe things for the rest of us to live by without saying that that is what they are actually doing. They often talk about being cooperative and compromising on the issues; but unfortunately conservatives are usually the ones who end up capitulating. And oftentimes liberals paint themselves into a corner with seemingly no way out; like Clinton's definition of an ideologue. But as is often the case, the media do their best to remain silent about potential controversial issues or they mount a vigorous defense on behalf of their political friends until things get back to normal.

The Clinton speech that I have been referring to was supposed to have been a talk about *Securing the Common Good*. Sounds really noble and wonderful; but how do you begin to define such a phrase? There are too many ways that "good" can be defined; many of which are not even close to being common, let alone good. I will admit that there are basic fundamental necessities that we all need in life. However, if many of these supposed facts that Clinton speaks of actually happened, then why are there people who still lament about all the inequality among us?

It would stand to reason that if something like paying higher taxes was such a righteous endeavor for the "common good," that there would be no reason for it not being universally accepted by everyone! Most of the things espoused by Clinton and other liberals seem to make sense because they usually involve helping other people. But the reason they do not actually help people long term is because they do not create the incentive for the recipients of practically any social program aimed at the "public good" to change the way they live.

Unfortunately, our fellow citizens in charge of running the government tend to find ways of wasting our tax dollars because they simply do not always have the best interests of the poor in mind, as is often the topic of their lectures. Usually, the result of paying more taxes to the government produces greater government waste and abuse, let alone the fact that it seems to engender a lack of ambition and motivation within the hearts and minds of the very people it is designed to benefit! Do we need additional proof that liberal policies like higher taxes have not worked over the last 100 years? Liberals would have us believe that when they are in charge, all poverty has a better chance of being eliminated.

Liberals have had their opportunity to eliminate poverty along with every other social ill and it seems they have had very little success. But it has still been difficult for republicans to overcome because those espousing liberal policies have been successful using emotion to convince listeners that their philosophy is better for the people. And when emotion trumps common sense, reason is often discarded. Take a look at the direction our "free market" is headed—under government control, primarily because conservatives have not been doing what it takes to educate the electorate. There is no government program now, or ever, that is sufficient to raise people out of poverty or provide for the people in any other way no matter what politicians say; yet we are to believe that the Clinton administration led people out of poverty, to the tune of "2 million children?"

Generally speaking, presidents get entirely too much credit for things they have no real control over; this certainly applies to Clinton and every other president as well. Congress should receive an equal share of the credit when sensible legislation has been passed—as well as appropriate blame if stupidity rules the day. The president can always make himself look good by signing wise legislation into law, even though he may be ridiculed for it. But by the same token the president can be on the wrong side of the people if he does not make wise use of the veto pen, as in the case of health care.

As for the judicial branch, perhaps it can best be said that, "In the legislative and executive branches, it's acceptable ... to make decisions based on your personal opinions and interests. The role of a judge, by contrast, is to interpret and apply the choices made in those branches, not to make policy choices of his own."[61] Amen! Sonia Sotomayor could learn a thing or two from Supreme Court Justice Clarence Thomas about making decisions based upon the law, not based on her social experiences as a Hispanic woman.

It seems that liberal government should have taken care of inequality and eradicated it from our lives by now, at least since the 1990s if the policies and beliefs of people like Bill Clinton are really that extraordinary! I suppose that in the post-Clinton era, we are left to conclude that government run by liberals is not the answer to what plagues America, even though Mr. Obama is leading the charge for an unprecedented liberal government revival like no other.

If only Al Gore could have won in 2000 so that all the progressive momentum that Clinton initiated and presided over could have had a chance to flourish. That Bush character is to blame for ruining everything, including anything that Obama has tried to do because, after all, he inherited the worst crises since the Great Depression, not to mention the "war on terror." It was Mr. Clinton that said: "For me, the ultimate test is not whether the intellectual architecture of my view as opposed to the view of those that are running things now [meaning Bush] is more pristine and less messy, but whether people are going to be better off when you quit than when you started."[62] By better off, I guess he was talking about people recognizing how much better off they are when dependent upon government instead of investing in the struggle to be independent of the government. Naturally, the country was so much better off when Clinton was president than at any other time in history, which would mean that Clinton, of all people, should be in love with the scope and power of an Obama administration, whose aim seems to be that every person that has a chance to be born is taken care of until the day they die.

It is probably safe to believe that in America there will probably always be those who are seemingly stuck on the bottom rung of the ladder; and for some, they may be content to remain there due to their own lack of desire to work. But if you want to progress to the next rung the only person holding you back is you. Each individual who has the capacity must decide what part of the ladder they want to occupy; not the government, a teacher, your Mom or Bill Clinton. The motivation and will to progress and succeed is not something that government can provide. On the contrary, it seems that government, and more specifically, liberal government seeks to keep people dependent on it, as opposed to helping people remove the shackles or barriers to success and real freedom. If government is the answer to getting people off the lower rungs of the ladder, I imagine that a master plan would have been devised and implemented by now. We know that the social model implemented and tried beginning in earnest with FDR was a failed policy that the Democratic Party and liberals are unwilling to extricate themselves.

Mr. Obama is going to great lengths to encompass all the aspects of so many failed policies from the past, and then some. The one thing well-intentioned people like Clinton and Obama fail to realize is that it is not up to government to determine how successful its citizens will be. Indeed, no amount of pushing, pulling, or dragging anyone to a higher rung on the ladder is going to guarantee success at any other rung, because the government does not, nor indeed, cannot produce the personal motivation and responsibility. I would like to know what great blessings have rained down upon the heads of the people because of government-sponsored social programs from the last 100 years, other than government dependency. Of course, liberals are exceptionally giddy when as many of the people as possible subscribe to dependency, because in their minds that gives cause to the idea that we actually need them.

Every election cycle we seem to always hear the same old class warfare rhetoric about the disparity of the "haves" and the "have nots." Remember, government cannot run the private sector nor create success for its people; it has been tried before with pitiful results, which makes the things Obama is trying to do even more incredible. Government has its place, and too often the people who run it forget from whom they have received their authority. Conservatives and conservative republicans typically do not do a real good job of articulating the differences between those in our society who are in need of assistance from the government because of disability, and those who have no physical or mental handicaps yet manage to scam and cheat the government for all they can get. Like you, I have no need for the people in our country that attempt to get something for nothing. Of course, there are legitimate reasons for government assistance to some of our most vulnerable citizens; and anyone who believes that the government should turn its back on those not able to provide for themselves has no heart.

But government should also provide the necessary incentives so that businesses, for instance, can stay in America and continue to provide the jobs that will allow those on the lower rungs to progress on the economic ladder. The key to incentives is that government must keep tax rates low for all the people. If the people are able to keep more of their hard-earned money, they will have the incentive to save and invest; and consequently, raise themselves out of poverty while government observes from a safe distance. And like any household, the government must control spending and use the funds given to it by the people in the most judicious manner. It is not the government's job to save and invest for its citizens.

Ever since leaving office, Mr. Clinton has taken the opportunity to let people know that he is now counted among the elite in this country. "To achieve the common good, you have to believe in equal opportunity ... I never had any money till I left the White House, and now I'm one of those really important people. I'm a millionaire."[63] Actually, I would never fault the former president for taking advantage of American capitalism. I think it is great that Mr. Clinton is able to command top dollar for speaking engagements. As long as there is a demand for such things, the market will supply. In America, we call that the free market. I believe, however, that if he is so concerned about all the tax breaks he was receiving under the Bush administration, that if he feels he is "getting over" on the government, by all means he should be sending some extra cash to Uncle Sam; and for all I know, perhaps he is. It is also interesting to note his use of the phrase "equal opportunity" as it relates to the "common good." Equal opportunity in the United States is no longer viewed only in a theoretical sense by particular classes of people, but opportunity abounds for anyone ambitious enough to make their own way in twenty-first century America.

The challenge that Mr. Clinton and other like-minded individuals seem to face is that they believe that equal opportunity and the end result are one and the same. In other words, if the liberal philosophy is that not enough of the right people are experiencing the kind of success that they believe the right people are entitled to; then equal opportunity has not been achieved. This is part of the problem that is perpetuated by the insidious nature of quotas, affirmative action, and other government mandated programs that insist that one particular group is entitled to something above and beyond what the other is not. Unfortunately, there are no guarantees in this life as the opportunity to fail is just as much a part of the equation as the potential to succeed; but the opportunities are available to all.

The outcome of our opportunities depends on what we do, that is the only thing we control. We often hear people talk about getting the breaks and being lucky when it comes to success, but the bottom line in life is that we cannot rely on "the breaks" or being "lucky," to succeed. One thing is certain, however, failure is the only guarantee anyone can be certain of, but there is no rule that says that is where you have to remain.

I have never known government to motivate anyone in the private sector to succeed. Moreover, government seems to have a unique capacity for making people dependent, in hopes of fostering the "you need us" mentality. When politicians tell the American people all the things that they are going to do for them, we should recognize such talk as a moment to be doubtful and extremely wary. Instead of trying to find out what it is the people want, politicians just tell us what they think we want to hear, all of which is designed to garner the most possible votes. Both democrats and republicans engage in this disgusting behavior, and unfortunately, many people buy into such hypnotic rhetoric.

Everyone has their own definition of the meaning of success, and I can almost guarantee that the overwhelming majority of people in America do not set their goals for success based on what they are told by a politician. If you have been brainwashed into believing that your life will be better by voting for a particular politician because of incredibly unbelievable promises that they have made: beware! We have an obligation as voters to be extremely cautious and skeptical when we hear politicians use phrases such as: *Trust me; I promise; The fact of the matter is; Believe me; I'm not a crook; You can count on me; Let me be perfectly clear; Read my lips;* and the all time greatest, *I did not have sexual relations with that woman.*

I think that most of us want to believe in our elected officials, but sometimes it is difficult when all we have to rely on is past performance as a guide. There is too much cynicism among average citizens regarding politicians today; we need not imagine why. I do not believe we are being too simplistic when we demand that those seeking to represent us simply carry out campaign promises and stay away from over-promising and under-delivering. The trend of hollow promises often continues while in office. I do not need to be lectured by anyone about the fact that the reason many people seek elected office today is for the purpose of gaining power; even though there is nothing inherently corrupt with power itself. However, most people who become politicians are not equipped to handle the kind of power bestowed upon them as a result of winning an election, power that leads to the potential for corruption. Therefore, the lust for power often distorts the true motive that should prevail when one seeks political office, which is to be a servant to the people.

There is a troubling trend that seems to prevail in many circles of our society today. Not only are a lot of citizens becoming complacent and indifferent to what happens in politics, but many have also become too apathetic to care if a politician is truthful or not in his communication. Too many of us often adopt the attitude that "they all do it," meaning that all politicians lie, so our job is to pick the one who is the most charismatic or is better at appearing to be truthful compared to his opponent. And unfortunately, it seems that believability is not even that important anymore. Whether you believe a politician is going to give you a handout or do whatever he can to get out of your life so you can achieve success as you define it; we will more than likely vote for the person we think is going to adhere to our philosophy.

Unfortunately, there are people in life who define success by how much they can "get" for nothing in return; and power-hungry politicians do all they can to secure the vote of such a particular block. Through education, it is up to average folks like me and you to change the hearts and minds of those who define success based on what a politician says he will do for them. It is time for conservatives to start focusing on the deceitful terms used by liberals to define "progress" for the rest of us. Liberals seem to believe that those who do not support progressivism as they define it must be against equality for all. That belief is simply untrue, and in reality, true conservatives simply believe that right and wrong exists in the world and do not believe it to be "progressive" to kill an unborn fetus or recognize same sex marriage , for instance. I would imagine if an unborn child were able to express it, he or she would be "pro choice" when it comes to living or not. And just because I may be against same sex couples marrying does not mean that I think they are any less equal.

The Declaration of Independence was an inspired document, one that led to our sovereignty as a nation. Furthermore, it is a model for all citizens to realize that they can break free from the oppression of elected leaders in a Republic. Although it would be a stretch to define some of our entrenched leaders in Washington, D.C., as tyrannical, it is easy to make such comparisons when it comes to various aspects of life such as taxation and superfluous governmental regulatory control. After all, what is a tyrant but one who has the ability to make life miserable for those subjected to his will? A productive life of complete independence must be free from the coercion of one who is elected to public office, because when limited government reigns, there is greater access to the whole pie, indeed there is plenty of it to go around in our capitalistic system. The task is to figure out how to keep government hands out of it, and never supporting anyone who would apologize to the rest of the world because of a system in America that is unlike any in the entire world.

FREEDOM AND ENGLISH

Here is one of those unwritten laws that most of us are familiar with: "My freedom is sacrificed at the moment my fist meets your nose." I am sure we have all heard a similar phrase to some degree or another. And most of us have probably either been on the receiving end or the retaliatory side, or perhaps both. The bottom line is that freedom is not free. As Americans, we need to be aware of the costs of the freedom we cherish. Possibly the most sought after human aspiration is the longing to be able to enjoy freedom; indeed, we accept it as inalienable. Certainly, every person blessed to live in the United States accepts the reality of doing whatever they desire within the bounds of the law, and without fear of retribution from the government. America is truly a blessed country! In spite of some of the negative press from the media about how evil America is portrayed by people outside the country, there are still plenty of people trying to make their way here in the hope of improving their circumstances. Yes, there are even those who have made their way to America to do us harm; and still others who consider it a challenge to infiltrate our porous borders with the intent of doing us harm, so it is safe to say that we are beyond the point of action when it comes to securing our borders.

Of all the nations conceived by man and blessed by God, the United States of America stands as the model of freedom and independence to the world. It does not matter that there is reluctance by some to admit this fact, or not acknowledge it altogether; however, it is a fact, like night following the day. Since our founding, there has always been a price to pay to secure our liberty. A lot of young people today have very little appreciation for the sacrifices that so many have made who preceded them in mortality. As a nation, we are losing the WWII generation, of which my father-in-law, John C. Wyeth II, was a part, and for whom my family honored, with the rest of his family and friends at a memorial service to commemorate his passing on March 17, 2009.

John was one of many quiet dignified heroes of his generation for which this nation owes a debt of gratitude that we can never repay. From the infancy of our independence to the current war against radical, extreme, and hate-filled terrorists; men and women of our nation have always answered the call of duty. And in case there may be those who doubt the resolve of Americans, please understand that we do not take freedom for granted and an ever-present vigilance is needed now, more than ever, to defeat any who wish to do America harm.

Those who signed the Declaration of Independence had this to say in the face of unjustified rule: "The history of the present King of Great Britain is a history of repeated injuries and usurpations, all having in direct object the establishment of an absolute Tyranny over these States."[64] Since the desire for independence, America has been a nation unwilling to yield to tyrants, kings, dictators, or terrorists. And those elected to serve the people by defending the Constitution had better never forget it. Unlike many leaders of nations that seek dominance by absolute power, typically in the United States, we do not elect leaders who impose the will of America upon other nations by conquer and conquest. Today, it is not necessarily the threats we face from other nations, though that is always a real possibility, but we seem to face greater challenges from radicals like the Taliban, who reside within those nations.

The U.S. has been involved in its share of conflicts; however, no reasonably thinking individual can accuse this country of attempting to control the destiny of other nations, though other nations have been guilty of such actions in the world. The nobility and goodness of America must be shouted from the rooftops! It must be done, however, with humility and appreciation, not arrogance and ingratitude. I believe we need to be reminded on a regular basis of all the good that America has accomplished throughout the world. We do not need the president travelling overseas to apologize for what he seems to think are the sins of America. All I can say to anyone that thinks America needs to apologize is this: try leaving the country and living in a place like Cuba, Venezuela, or any other third world country and perhaps you will have a renewed perspective and appreciation for what America means to the rest of the world. I am tired of people in our country apologizing for what they think America has done to the rest of the world. We are only weakened in the eyes of our enemies when this kind of attitude prevails.

I do not believe it to be coincidental that a relatively small band of men were concentrated in the same place, at the same moment in history. The hand of providence was unquestionably upon the historic figures we know as the founding fathers, whose purpose was not only to conceive a new nation; but draft the articles that were later ratified as the Declaration of Independence and Constitution. The blessing of liberty has even been extended to those who have come to this country illegally because politicians are afraid to address the issue of immigration for fear they will lose at the ballot box next time around. Well, that attitude is an insult to anyone who works to secure our borders or who has died doing so. It is also an insult to anyone who has ever lost a loved one in war—from the current "war on terror" to the Revolution. Why don't these politicians wake up and realize that it is not about them, that it is not just politics, but that they need to use all means necessary to protect American lives? Their job is to protect, preserve and defend the Constitution.

The founding fathers believed that "Prudence ... will dictate that governments long established should not be changed for light and transient causes; and accordingly all experience hath shown, that mankind are more disposed to suffer, while evils are sufferable, than to right themselves by abolishing the forms to which they are accustomed."[65] Our founding fathers could endure; indeed they did endure various "evils" imposed by Great Britain. They were forced to endure under the hands of a tyrant until, united in determination and fortitude, they were able to abolish a form of government to which they had been accustomed; and under which they had been "disposed to suffer." Make no mistake about it; the men who signed the Declaration and drafted the Constitution were willing to put their lives in jeopardy to abolish a "form" of government that was restrictive, coercive, and tyrannical. The outcome of their decisions and subsequent resolve has blessed the lives of countless millions.

The founding fathers understood the need for governmental power to be dispersed, not concentrated in the hands of a few or even one. Everyone has the freedom to believe as they wish, but when it comes to the establishment of the United States, mere coincidence could not have been a part of the equation. Our form of government continues today because of the grace of God and through principles outlined and upheld in the Declaration of Independence and Constitution, and because of the strength and determination of a military that is second to none. We cannot afford to be passive or apathetic when it comes to issues like securing our borders; our politicians have to be aggressive in order to protect the people, and they need not worry about offending anyone because of it. We have been blessed by the hand of God for over two-hundred and thirty years. Unfortunately, that blessing may be in jeopardy because of prowling, power-hungry politicians who only care about themselves and presumably advancing their status among the people. As a nation, we cannot afford to be at the mercy of those who do not have the best interests of the people at heart.

Whether liberals want to admit it or not, there have been efforts by a host of supposed freedom-loving people who want to have God taken out of the public discourse. I have never really understood such rationale. And it is not only that, but I think we could all agree that our neglect to exemplify god-like qualities such as love, kindness, and goodness have led to a more corrupt society; all because of the false premise that we do not want to offend those who may not believe in God. That approach is poison. For instance, we have all heard of efforts to have the Ten Commandments removed from Court Houses across the country, as well as in other "state" sanctioned areas.

What about efforts by some to have "In God We Trust" removed from our currency? And how long has it been since prayer was "officially" removed from the public school system? Imagine if young people in our public schools today were allowed to begin the day with an invocation; if it's good enough for Congress, then it ought to be good enough for students in the public school system. Perhaps allowing our students to pray vocally in school would do more to curtail disrespect for authority and the general lack of respect evident among some of our young people today. There are certainly plenty examples in our society when the name of deity is trampled upon all in the name of "freedom of speech," yet young people are sometimes ridiculed for even professing a desire to be able to have school-wide prayer. Those against such things seem to be under the mistaken notion that praying in school is somehow mingling religion with education. I would simply say that such people do not have a right to prohibit those who want to see school-wide prayer become an acceptable practice in public schools.

Our country was founded upon centuries-old Judeo-Christian principles and has evolved into a very tolerant nation when it comes to accepting the tenants of any other religion. Yet there seems to be a relatively small minority with no shame or apologies for pushing such time-tested values out of the public square all for the supposed purpose of not offending those who choose to believe differently. We must be aware of those who want to eliminate the free expression of religion in America that does not injure or harm someone else.

Why should the vast majority of people in this country be made to feel guilty by a few, because of our Judeo-Christian heritage? The few who do not like the facts of our founding can always go somewhere else to live; and good luck trying to get another nation to be as tolerant and sympathetic as America. Can you imagine living in a country where the dominant religion was anything but Judeo-Christian? In many other countries, there are "state" religions that make it next to impossible for someone who may be of another religion to practice their faith the way they see fit. As I recall, we have a dandy little provision in our Constitution that makes "state" controlled religion in this country illegal. Coercion and religion are not usually compatible, and if used as a means of increasing converts, will probably not help a congregation to grow. In America, we let people believe what they choose, even if someone is "forced" to listen to a prayer at school. Besides, the mere saying of a prayer in a public place usually does not lead to someone converting, and even though we may not understand or even accept a particular religion, we extend to all the right to worship as they see fit.

Had the nineteen hijackers responsible for the September 11, 2001, terrorists' attacks on our country had even a remote appreciation for the Ten Commandments, they would not have been disillusioned with the notion of attacking our country: "Thou shalt not kill; Thou shalt not bear false witness against thy neighbor; Thou shalt not covet."[66] The Ten Commandments are a great place for anyone to build the foundation of a life committed to treating others the way we would like to be treated.

A typical prayer offered at a Christian church on a given Sunday is something that tends to inspire compassion and devotion, and softens the hearts of listeners. We can all probably agree that a softening of the heart is a good thing, considering the coarseness that seems prevalent in our society today. Frankly, I have never understood the notion that the type of language used while praying is somehow offensive, unless it

139

is inspired by a selfish agenda. The mere offering of a prayer in a public setting does not restrict someone who may not be Christian, or diminish their religion or their right to worship. I suspect that an objection to prayer in a public setting might be motivated by people who harbor ill will toward Christians; indeed, who have a hidden agenda other than their concern for "separation of church and state."

If I were to go to a predominantly non-Christian country, I would be expected to be respectful of a religion and tolerate it, even though I may not subscribe to it. This fact does not diminish my Christian beliefs, even if the method of prayer is completely unlike what I am used to. I certainly would not take action to aggressively protest against the principal non-Christian religion of another country. A major impetus for the establishment of America was the concept for the expression of religious freedom. Anyone desiring to make the United States their home should be prepared to at least tolerate Christianity. And for those that have lived here all their lives, who may not be Christian, please understand the significance of Judeo-Christian teachings and tolerate the fact that such principles can be demonstrated without infringing upon your right to worship the way you see fit. And certainly Christians must lead by example and be tolerant of those that may not believe as they do.

It seems that we have been reduced by a small minority in this country to a form of political expediency and political correctness. We have discussed previously some of the politically expedient decisions made by elected office holders and sanctioned by some of the people in this country. It is no secret that politicians today will say whatever they need to say to get elected; a far cry from the days of our founding. Oh, sure, politicians today talk about the sanctity of public service and about how noble it is to be involved in such an endeavor; but do you ever notice how they seem to be the only people who talk about public service in such noble terms? I do not doubt that public service is truly noble, but it would seem that if it were so noble, more of the rest of us would talk about it in equally glowing terminology. Nobility is measured by actions, not words.

There seems to be quite a bit of difference between the nobility of a Benjamin Franklin or Abraham Lincoln compared to that of some of our most notable politicians today. I would never question another's piety, nor do I believe that all our founding fathers lived saintly lives. But something tells me that if Abraham Lincoln ever invoked the blessings of God upon his listeners, that he was sincere and spoke from the heart, without ulterior motives. Today, when most politicians use the phrase, "God bless you," or "God bless America," it seems to be nothing more than a worn-out cliché. And naturally, it is acceptable to have a politician invoking the blessings of God upon those within the sound of their voice; they just do not want a student or teacher at a public school invoking similar blessings by offering a school-wide prayer to God during school hours or at a commencement, for instance. Make no mistake about it; there is an element in our society that will stop at nothing to have the name of God stricken from every state, federal, and nationally recognized site in the country; and on deck, the effort to impose a penalty against anyone who mentions the name of God in public or tries to practice the tenants of their religion, whether in public or in the privacy of their own home; certainly a far cry from the days of our founding.

In San Diego County, California, a pastor and his wife were questioned by a county employee for conducting informal meetings in their own home, and who in fact "notified the couple that the small Bible study, with an average of fifteen people attending, was in violation of county regulations ... the couple received a written warning that listed [unlawful use of land] and told them to [stop religious assembly or apply for a major use permit]—a process that could cost tens of thousands of dollars."[67]

The idea that American citizens could be punished for mentioning the name of God in a public setting may not appear as extreme anymore, considering the boldness of the San Diego County experience of private citizens. I guess it comes down to the fact that it only matters how the name of God is used. It seems to be acceptable to take the name of God in vain in places like the halls of Congress, the movies, on TV, at school, or work; and no one seems to care too much about that.

In the meantime, in a relatively short period of time, we have devolved as a society that once believed that it was inappropriate to take the name of God in vain in practically any public setting, and certainly not in the presence of a lady, to a society where it has become quite fashionable to irreverently use the name of God in vain anywhere and in front of anybody. Not only does it seem fashionable, but it is quite acceptable as well. And not many people seem to care; although, I imagine God does. Once again, a quote from the Ten Commandments seems appropriate: "Thou shalt not take the name of the Lord thy God in vain."[68]

It is interesting to note that the Ten Commandments are not necessarily an endorsement of Christianity, though they are indeed central to Christian faith. The Ten Commandments are simply a blueprint for the quest to live a good life no matter the religion or society, though it may not always seem like doing good or being good is in vogue or fashionable.

At what point do "we the people" begin to exclaim that our liberties seem to be getting curtailed at the expense of an extreme minority? Naturally, anyone with a particular belief or set of values, that when curtailed or limited altogether, will embrace the urge to defend their cause in a movement that is bigger than themselves to ensure that "rights" are not restricted. For me to believe that I have a "right" to do what I please, even if it means that someone else could be injured or hurt by my actions is ludicrous. But there are rights that have been designated as inalienable, and the first ten Amendments to the Constitution, the Bill of Rights, are no exception. Contained within the First Amendment is the fact that the people have the right to the "free exercise"[69] of religion, among other things.

Speaking primarily within the context of God, and not necessarily religion, the right of the people to pray vocally to God in a public setting should never have been taken away in our society to the extent that it has been. God is not a religion, per se. The majority of the founding fathers shared a belief in God to some degree or another; and most of them, indeed, had a profound respect for God, though they may have had varying "religious" beliefs. So I ask: why was prayer to God taken out of our public schools to the extent that it has been since we were granted the "free exercise" of religion by the Constitution? Does the government have the right to infringe upon my right to the "free exercise" of religion simply because I'm at school? It seems that praying vocally in school has nothing to do with the idea that "Congress shall make no law respecting an establishment of religion." Instead, a small minority have taken it upon themselves the liberal interpretation that vocal prayer in school is somehow equivalent to the "establishment of religion."

There will always be those who will attempt to rationalize that religion and prayer in a public setting is much too complex for an unlearned, inexperienced, and untrained person in the law such as myself. These sophists probably assume that an average American is just not as refined a progressive as themselves to understand the multifaceted intricacies and implications of religion and prayer in public settings as it relates to the law. Frankly, a healthy batch of common sense is a good remedy, and much needed today. Too often, we seem to only hear from the people who are recognized as "authoritative" when it comes to speaking on matters of legal importance. Yes, we need people to understand law, but what we have today are a bunch of people who have to try and figure out how to best manipulate the law to bend in their favor.

The irony is that even though the principle of "freedom of religion" was an essential element of our founding; it is indeed one of the "rights" that seem to draw so much attention by those concerned that when their kids go to school, that it may lead to the next revival. But often, the attention is focused on what can be done to shame, primarily Christians into feeling that they owe the world an apology for simply practicing their religion. But on the other hand it seems that great effort is made by many in public service and the media to avoid criticizing Islam because that would not be considered the moral high ground. I guess the assumption is that Christians are a more submissive and forgiving target.

Unfortunately, apologetic rhetoric sometimes actually comes from within the ranks of Christians, for instance, when prior to giving the prayer at the Lincoln Memorial for an inaugural event for then President-elect Obama, Episcopal Bishop Gene Robinson said that he did not know what he would say; only that he wouldn't use the Bible. He said, "While that is a holy and sacred text to me, it is not for many Americans. I will be careful not to be especially Christian in my prayer. This is a prayer for the whole nation."[70] Here is a classic example of a Christian who seems more concerned about political correctness than enjoying the freedom to practice his religion.

It seems to me that the Bishop's unwillingness to use the Bible as "a holy and sacred text" is a complete disregard to the pattern for prayer given to us from the Bible: "The Lord's Prayer." To my knowledge, I do not recall a time when Jesus ever apologized for teaching His followers how to pray. Devoted Christians cannot afford to be passive when it comes to defending their right to pray vocally in public, using scripture as a guideline. I would imagine that we could expect much different behavior from a devout Jew or Muslim with regard to how they might use their holy texts as a pattern for prayer; and I dare say that even most Christians would have had a different approach than that of Bishop Robinson, under similar circumstances.

If a handful of supposedly well-intentioned people are able to steal away the rights of a majority (Christians) they may not be content to stop there. I imagine that if such movements proved unsuccessful in curtailing a particular right from the Bill of Rights, then the only thing remaining is to attack the very document upon which our freedom has come, and from which the Bill of Rights sprang—yes, the Constitution. I realize that it seems like a ludicrous proposition, but stay with me for a moment. It is, or should be common knowledge (common sense) that at the time of the establishment of the American colonies that the King of Great Britain, as well as a host of other people, not the least of which were British troops themselves, probably underestimated the eventual success of the colonists. Not even the king or anyone clinging to the mother country had the slightest inkling that a new nation would eventually be conceived. The point I am making here is that a new nation was not to be denied to a people that had the determination to see their freedom become a reality. The same can be said of efforts by some to restrict any of our rights today, that there are factions in existence, even among government leaders, who are equally determined to subvert our rights as American citizens.

It does not matter if we are talking about religious rights or any other right that could be taken away. If it's religious rights today, what will it be tomorrow? What about all the other rights we enjoy as outlined by the Bill of Rights? What kinds of things would have to happen in order for the foundation of our rights in the United States to be vulnerable? It simply comes down to embracing the attitude framed by Edmund Burke, who said that, "No one could make a greater mistake than he who did nothing because he could do only a little." One of the greatest mistakes our country could make at any time in the future is to go back to the pre-September 11, 2001, mentality that we are under no threat from our enemies.

The first attack on The World Trade Center in 1993 should have been enough of a wake-up call to the people in our government at that time; but obviously there were too many people who were afraid to go after the perpetrators the way we should have because it seemed that the administration at the time wanted to use the approach of the legal system as opposed to any sort of military offensive. Make no mistake about it; there will always be those who continue to plot ways to destroy our way of life, whether from within or outside the country.

It may not be the politically correct thing to say but we must be concerned about threats to our liberty from within the country. I speak of the threats that may even come from within the halls of Congress. I do not support, nor am I sympathetic to the citizen "whack jobs" that stash guns, ammo, grenades, or bomb making materials, just waiting for the right moment to bring down a corner of the nation. I am speaking from the perspective of a concerned citizen that does not want to see the country he loves reduced to a mere parenthetical note in a history book because the people in charge failed to take seriously their responsibility to protect us. And if you love your country and support the military the way I do; I imagine that you share my passion. I will defend what is rightfully mine with every ounce of energy I possess. As a people, we not only have to be aware of the kinds of weapons that kill and maim physically, but also the kinds of weapons government wields through the pen and the dissemination of ideas.

I have mentioned previously the fact that I am an optimist. I tend to see the glass as being half full, not half empty. This does not mean, however, that optimist's are gullible or naïve when it comes to those who, by their very nature, are evil and cunning, who harbor nefarious ideas while waiting for the opportune time to bring them to light. Contrary to the conventional wisdom that seemed to prevail after 9/11, we do not all speak with one voice when it comes to matters of protecting this country. For instance, it may have seemed like everyone was unified after 9/11, but we all witnessed how that misguided belief disappeared in a relatively short period of time.

Having said that, I think it is extremely irresponsible to believe that there are relatively few threats to our freedom from within the country, and that unless like-minded people come together, misery and chaos could be the outcome. Edmund Burke also made this very popular statement: "All that is necessary for the triumph of evil is that good men do nothing." I am not necessarily saying that there are evil people in the Congress or other branches of government; but what I am saying is that the results of liberal political thinking usually means that the consequences to our freedom are not good for America.

During the height of the war in Iraq there were many prominent members of Congress (Dick Durbin, Harry Reid, and John Kerry) who did more than legitimately question our role and character there, as well as portraying Guantanamo Bay as something other than what it is. Some of the things they said undermined our efforts to prosecute the war and were counterproductive to troop morale, such as this from Durbin: "If I read this to you and didn't tell you that it was an FBI agent describing what Americans had done to prisoners in their control, you would most certainly believe this must have happened by Nazis, Soviets in their gulags, or some mad regime, Pol-Pot or others, that had no concern for human beings. Sadly, that's not the case. This was the action of Americans in treatment of our—their own prisoners."[71]

Or how about this one from Reid: "I believe that the Secretary of State, Secretary of Defense and—you have to make your own decisions as to what the president knows—this war is lost and the surge is not accomplishing anything as indicated by the extreme violence in Iraq…"[72] This from the Senate Majority Leader!

And how about this from Kerry: "And there is no reason…that young American soldiers need to be going into the homes of Iraqis in the dead of night, terrorizing kids and children, you know, women…"[73] Such comments are beyond irresponsible by those who have been elected to represent the people. And please do not tell me that conservatives make the same sort of comments. Anyone would be hard-pressed to find a conservative who has made equally irresponsible comments disparaging our troops and their efforts in the War on Terror.

What happened to people like Durbin, Kerry, and Reid for making such comments? Were they reprimanded or censured? Unfortunately they were not, because politicians often believe they are above reproach. We must do all we can to change the culture in Washington and hold our elected representatives accountable for what they say or do. "We the people" deserve nothing less than every single politician doing what they were elected to do: represent our interests and certainly support our troops. We do not need the Reid's, Durbin's, and Kerry's of the world to use language that does nothing but incite the people to be continually divided over the things that we should be united in overcoming. If these kinds of politicians are spewing this sort of inflammatory language in public about such weighty matters, I cannot imagine the kinds of things they might be holding back.

Here is something you may or may not consider a threat to our freedom: English! And before anyone gets excited to the point of hysteria, this is not an anti-immigration position or a rant-filled hate barrage aimed at anyone living in the US who does not speak the language. Let me preface everything I happen to say about speaking English hereafter by stating that I have absolutely nothing against anyone that can speak another language or anyone migrating to this country legally. First of all, I think it is great if you can speak another language besides English, really. As a matter of fact, two of my children and a son-in-law speak Spanish, as well as a second son-in-law who speaks fluent French. I suppose if I were motivated, I would probably learn to speak another language as well. However, since I am not planning on living abroad any time soon, English seems to be serving me well for the time being. As a matter of fact, while living in Germany many years ago, I made the effort to speak as much Deutsche as I could whenever speaking with a native. And in the few years we lived there, I got by in situations where I needed to use the language. Had my wife and I made the decision to make Germany our permanent home, as painstaking as it would have been for me, I would have learned to speak the language so that I could have assimilated into the culture as opposed to expecting my German hosts to adapt to my English.

You may be wondering what all this has to do with being a threat to our freedom. For starters, we were decisive in a couple of wars that, had we not won—well, use your imagination. In other words, there is a reason why English is the language of the United States. There is also a reason why English is referred to as the "universal language," and why our country is the United States of America—not a collection of European-type countries. After the establishment of the colonies and the eventual organization of the states, immigrants began to flock to the US in ever increasing numbers. Upon arrival, immigrants assimilated into the culture and adopted English as their language. English became the official language of the several states and did not have to be mandated by the government because it was common knowledge that along with a new country, a common language became the binding tie; a new culture was evolving.

It did not matter if you were Italian, German, French, or African; eventually you learned to speak English if you wanted to become part of the culture (melting pot). It seems ridiculous that debate has surfaced in the past regarding the idea of making English the official language of the country, granted it has not been much of a debate. But it has obviously been a topic of discussion, perhaps because of the unwillingness of some immigrants to speak the English language. And for those living here and who get along fine without speaking English, obviously, I would not be talking about them. But please do not denigrate those of us who may be concerned about the time, effort, and money being spent to accommodate those too apathetic to learn English.

Please understand that besides members of my own family, I have an array of friends who speak a myriad of languages, and

I have nothing but profound respect for such ability. But guess what? Those same friends speak English fluently, too. Unfortunately, it seems like our country has evolved into a nation that by the time I have grandchildren old enough to go to college, the US may not be a predominantly English speaking country. Why would I have a problem with that? English is an identifiable characteristic of American culture; it's one of those things that provide commonality. People all over the world learn English. Why do you suppose that so many people across the planet learn a secondary language to the degree that English is mastered and spoken? It is really quite simple and can be summed up in three letters: USA! Whether it is popular to admit or not, people all over the world want to be able to deal with America in a number of ways. Regardless of what some, even in this country, want us to believe, we are still the envy of the free world, even though a lot of people have tried to drive this country into the ground politically, economically, socially, and morally.

I have had the opportunity of living in several different states. But like many other places in the country, in certain corners English seems to be rapidly becoming a secondary language instead of the predominant language. I cannot stress the significance of how incredible I think it would be to be able to speak another language; but when it becomes necessary for people in the medical or insurance fields, for instance, to hire interpreters so that doctors and nurses can have their patients understand something as crucial as their own health; something is wrong. We should not have to create laws with the mandate that "health and dental plans supply interpreters and translated material ... "[74] for patients. I believe it is the responsibility of every individual living in America to be accommodating when it comes to speaking the language; not the duty of a state or any other government entity to provide accommodative services.

As with a lot of things in life, there are exceptions. If you are taking care of an elderly parent or individual, for instance, who never took the time to learn English or simply came to this country late in life, it seems impractical, and would probably be unreasonable for someone like that to learn English now, though they still could. Common sense should always prevail.

It does not seem reasonable to expect our government to spend millions of taxpayer dollars every year catering to speakers of other languages because some do not want to put forth the effort to learn the language. For instance, why should we print ballots for elections in any other language than English? It ought to be required to learn enough English so that exercising the right to vote in this country can be appreciated as an honor and privilege, not necessarily a right. We are surrounded by the "fairness" crowd that always seems to question whether this or that is "fair" or not. Well, I do not think it is fair to make translations in Spanish only. What about all the other languages that people speak who live in the US? Is it fair to them that their native tongue is not included on an election ballot? I'm well aware that compared to every other language, Spanish is probably the most common foreign language spoken in the US; but if we are going to oblige native speakers of one language, we should do the same for every other language. Wouldn't that be "fair?"

The way to solve this dilemma and save time and money is by having everything in English only. What better way to motivate people to learn the language, at least to the proficiency of a fourth or fifth grader, which is probably sufficient for anyone to get by in America. The problem is that we have too many politicians who want to remove the incentive for people to learn the language. Think about it. If you are an immigrant living in America and your host nation bends over backward to remove your motivation to learn English; why bother learning it? I do not think that it is asking too much for an immigrant living here to learn the language. All of this talk leads me to one of the most controversial topics facing our nation today: the immigration of hundreds of thousands of people to this country through illegal means.

I believe that illegal immigration is one of the most serious challenges facing the freedom of our nation today, though consistent action has not been taken to eliminate it. I have absolutely nothing against those who come to this country via legal means. As with any controversial issue, being able to discuss the pros and cons of it in a civilized fashion are imperative to reaching any sort of resolution, and the only way to accomplish this is to do so with control, reason, and common sense. Too often, proponents of either side become overly sensitive and emotional beyond reason, so that nothing ever gets accomplished. It seems to me that most people fall into two camps with respect to the immigration question. One, there are those who believe that if foreigners want to come to this country, they should be allowed to do so, end of discussion. And two, there is the group that believes that foreigners have an opportunity to enter this country, indeed, are welcomed to do so by established legal means.

First, we need to briefly discuss the reason why this nation cannot simply allow people to enter into the country without first possessing the proper credentials. In a post 9/11 world, allowing anyone to come into the country illegally is unthinkable and should be a top priority of law enforcement and politicians since they are responsible for ensuring our safety. Yet, securing our borders does not seem to be a top priority of every politician. I suppose if it was not a top priority immediately following the terrorist attacks; then unfortunately, it might not be on the top of the list nearly ten years later as we still have inadequate security on our borders.

Whether foreigners visit our country on a work or education visa, or with the intention of making the US a permanent home, we must scrutinize every single person desiring to enter our country. We must not worry about whether we are being insensitive by simply doing what is within our right as a sovereign nation to do. I do not have anything against anyone wanting to come to this country seeking a better life. However, I think a lot of people have forgotten that the nineteen hijackers responsible for 9/11 by attacking our sovereignty, at least technically entered the country "legally."

Our government must be vigilant and examine the credentials of all who enter the country legally and we cannot afford to think differently or be soft about this topic; now or in the future. Frankly, it is disturbing that many in the "no questions asked … let them enter crowd" are probably many of the same people who get themselves worked up over racial profiling as well. These same people most likely accept the notion that America is guilty of past grievances against foreigners and should just let any and all of them come into the country. This attitude is dangerous.

We need to look at the illegal immigration argument from the standpoint of non-terrorists for a moment. Take a moment to think about all the riffraff, lawbreakers, and otherwise-less-than-desirables continually trying, and in many cases succeeding, in their attempt to make it across the border every day. Remember, we are talking about non-terrorists. Do we really want the drug dealers, drug runners, gang bangers, murderers, thugs, rapists, child abusers; and every other imaginable scum, crossing into the country when we already have too much of that sort of thing that is home grown? The infamous catch and release program has probably not done a lot of good when it comes to keeping criminals out of our country; not to mention the fact that it has sent the wrong message to would-be lawbreakers crossing the border illegally. Our court system seems to be crowded with people from our own country who break the law; we do not need it to be occupied by illegal's clogging things up as well.

And if some people get their way, it will soon be clogged with terror suspects as well. It is no secret that the Border Patrol needs to be strengthened and supported by every politician from coast to coast. We cannot afford to see the kind of treatment given to Ignacio Ramos and Jose Compean, the two

Border Patrol officers who were trying to do their job, but were convicted for shooting an illegal: a known drug smuggler!

Thankfully, President Bush commuted their sentences prior to his leaving office in January 2009. Compean and Ramos had received multi-year convictions and had served about two years prior to their commutations. Unfortunately, the president did not extend to them a pardon, which would have positioned them to be able to return to their jobs as Border Patrol Agents. Who could blame them for being bitter toward the government for the treatment they received, and not wanting to return to their jobs even if they could?

When the terrorist element is added to the equation, it is easy to see how imperative it is for our government to get tough on securing the borders. Securing the border is a national security issue that must be dealt with and maintained.

I am tired of hearing supporters of illegal immigration label those who do not think like they do as racists and bigots. If there is a certain element in the world that happens to fit the profile or looks like one who is known to carry out evil acts among our people, then I'm all for profiling. Does this mean that just because a person does not fit the mold for a particular crime, that he is as pure as the driven snow; of course not. Timothy McVeigh was as "white" as they come and home grown. Does anyone doubt his terroristic nature? Given the geographical location of his despicable act, I imagine law enforcement set their sites on anyone fitting the profile of an extremely disturbed person who may have had a vendetta against the government for one reason or another, regardless of his ethnicity.

Ultimately, we found out that the guy was an extreme example of someone with a serious mental problem. The McVeigh profile should not be taken for granted, however. Since money tends to corrupt those with low morals, it makes sense for law enforcement to scrutinize any suspicious characters, foreigners or otherwise, who wish to enter the country. As a matter of fact,

McVeigh was so disturbed that not even money was his motivation for carrying out such a heinous and cowardly act.

For all the other twisted minds out there with too much time on their hands and absolutely no morals or a conscience, who would like to hit the "lottery," it would not take a lot of effort for evil, patterned after one of the nineteen hijackers, to pay off a personality like McVeigh to carry out an evil act upon unsuspecting Americans. Under such a scenario, it would probably be even more difficult to catch such a person, since everyone knows all "white" people look alike and that they never get profiled anyway.

It is amazing to me that not everyone thinks alike when it comes to the safety and security of this nation. Throughout the Bush administration (especially after 9/11), liberals and others continuously lamented over "racial profiling." My contention relative to profiling has always been that if you have not done anything wrong, you have nothing to worry about. Obviously, there are exceptions and anything can be taken to the extreme. I do not want my civil liberties violated any more than the next person, regardless of ethnicity; but being able to identify a suspect requires that law enforcement have all the tools available to apprehend, question, detain, and then either release or charge a suspect.

We do not live in a perfect world, so there are going to be mistakes made; but that does not mean that we abandon common sense principles that will help keep the people of this nation safe from those who want to do us harm no matter where they are from. Obviously, I do not believe that government operatives or law enforcement personnel ought to have the latitude to infringe upon our rights just because they're bored. There is often a fine line between probable cause and abuse of civil liberties, but I do not think that we want to tie the hands of the very people whose job it is to keep us safe.

Do we have to wait for another attack on our country to show the terrorists that we are really unified against them? If not, we should deal with profiling, and at the same time prosecute those in law enforcement who abuse their authority or the system. But it makes no sense to paralyze the hand of law enforcement all because a few people take offense to profiling.

LIBERAL POLICIES, RACIAL CHALLENGES AND THE IMPORTANCE OF EDUCATION

Many of the people trying to make their living inside cocoons of make believe showed their true colors relating to President George W. Bush; members of the media led the way. I believe, however, that history will ultimately be kind to Bush, even though there are many people living now who harbor real hatred for him and love to blame him for all negative things that happened in the country, not only during his administration, but even now. It is amazing the amount of otherwise intelligent family or friends that I have talked to about Bush that have bought into the media's characterization of him. Incidentally, I do not recall a lot of liberals worrying about "hate speech" when it was directed toward Bush. I'm sure we could all find something from eight years of the Bush administration that was written or spoken that would qualify as "hate speech." The liberal ACLU did not seem to speak out in defense of Mr. Bush. I wonder why.

Even though there were no criminal acts carried out against George W. Bush, that does not negate the fact that he was hated. And even if a crime were committed against Bush, and "hate" was proven as a motive against him, I am against "hate crime" legislation, because as far as I'm concerned, all crime is motivated by hate and/or intolerance. Are we to accept that enforcement of laws in our country is so weak that we need to have "hate crimes legislation" just to enforce laws against assault, murder, or robbery for instance? Perhaps we have come to a point in our society where some in the legal profession have been able to manipulate the law through a "technicality" just so clients are treated more lenient, while victims of violent crime often have to witness the perpetrator walking free in far too many instances.

I've never understood the role of "hate crimes legislation," specifically the role it plays in the gathering of evidence. I guess we have admitted that we are incapable of punishing alleged criminals through the normal process of evidence gathering unless the motive of "hatred" is codified in the form of a statute. "Hate crimes legislation" seems unnecessary because we should be punishing alleged criminals to the fullest extent of the law, based on the evidence, regardless of motive. If there is concern about sentencing, then let's increase the sentencing structure of the law to the maximum extent possible to punish the offender. Whether it is believable or not, the natural evolution of "hate crimes" may eventually open the door to punishing, by indictment, those who have a differing political opinion, drive the wrong kind of car, or whatever; all because the "law" says it is permissible even if evidence of a crime is non-existent. If this attitude continues to find momentum "hate" will become the "new" evidence.

It seems to me that conservatives do not usually receive the benefit of the doubt that they usually extend to other people. I do not think that conservatism is a perfect way of life, but politically speaking, it seems like the best thing going if practiced and defended. In California, during the elections of 2008, there was a proposition on the ballot which sought to codify marriage in the State Constitution as being between one man and one woman so as to protect the institution of marriage. The measure, known as Proposition 8 was passed by the voters in California. As a resident of California at the time, I supported

Proposition 8 and volunteered some of my time and resources, as did many, many other concerned citizens, doing what we could to make sure those in our communities understood the meaning of the outcome of the proposition, as to its passage or not. Prior to the passage of Prop 8, as well as afterward, demonstrations and protests were held to demonize anyone who supported Prop 8, most of which came from the very people demanding acceptance and tolerance for their lifestyle choice.

It is interesting to note how homosexuals get away with referring to heterosexuals as homophobic—Barney Frank even referring to Supreme Court Justice Antonin Scalia as a "homophobe."[75] Yet it is virtually unheard of to hear heterosexuals characterize homosexuals as heterophobes. I do not know why that is the case, nor do I care, except to the extent that homosexuals are just as capable of being bigots as anyone else, but that seldom, or never, is discussed by anyone in the media as being legitimate. Conservatives typically do not demonize those who may not agree with them because they understand the importance of debate and disagreement in our Republic. But anyone who supported Prop 8 in California was characterized as hateful and intolerant just because they disagreed with those who were against Prop 8.

Once democrats took control of Congress in 2006, they were emblazoned with renewed confidence and the animus for Bush ratcheted up with each passing week. The evidence that they were unwilling to work with the president in a bipartisan way was obvious, even to the casual observer. Every slip of the tongue by Bush was an opportunity for liberals to display their orgy-like glee; believing that their intellect, at least in their own minds, far surpassed his. Yet, with the inauguration of Barack Obama it was not long before the press would be given an equal opportunity to be as fair with the forty-fourth president as they had been with the forty-third. The question lingered, however, as to whether or not members of the media were ready to play hardball with Mr. Obama, and predictably, we did not have to wait long to see the outcome of their "hardball." Turns out it has been nothing more than a harmless game of T-ball, because the mainstream media simply adore Obama too much.

Just two days after taking the oath of office (one day if you count the redo on Wednesday), President Obama signed four executive orders, one of which had to do with the closing down of terrorists' facilities at the Naval Base in Guantanamo Bay, Cuba, known as *Gitmo*. It was no secret that Mr. Obama had campaigned as a candidate to shut down Gitmo if elected president, and true to that promise, he barely had time to warm up a chair before following through on that one. Naturally, the signing of his first executive order was covered by all the major media outlets. However, the media failed to focus on the president's painful inability to be presidential. Picture in your minds eye the President of the United States sitting at a table flanked by supporters, signing his first executive orders, not exactly the time to elaborate on many of the details; but because of his lack of preparation, he had to defer to White House counsel, Greg Craig, on matters that he was unsure of with regard to a mildly specific point. I'm sorry, but the president does not seek the guidance of someone in the audience (counsel or not) during the signing ceremony of his executive orders; it does not look presidential!

I only mention this because we all know that had Bush committed a similar indiscretion, he would have been lampooned by every media outlet for looking like a buffoon for not knowing what the heck he was signing! And, in fact, he often was portrayed by the media as a buffoon during his eight years in Washington; but Obama got a pass, one of many he has received and will undoubtedly continue to receive from media outlets that look the other way when a liberal is in office. To me, it is a blatant example of the double standard that exists in the media today because of its preference for liberals and liberal policies. Even though Obama's signing of an Executive order is not policy, per se, his liberal philosophy with respect to Gitmo, manifested so quickly after taking the Oath of Office certainly portends of his liberal philosophy. Looking back it was certainly a sign of things to come given what we have witnessed during the first half of his presidency and the liberal policy driven agenda he has advocated. And obviously the signing of an executive order to close Gitmo has come to mean absolutely nothing.

During Bush's second term, many democrats, especially the radical wing of the party, lamented that America's standing amongst our friends in the world had been damaged by such a brazen "cowboy" president. They whined about his style. They were easily embarrassed and wished to show the world that we really were much more intelligent and sophisticated than the personification of stupidity they believed to be the substance of George W. Bush; especially coming on the heels of Bill Clinton, who could do no wrong in their jaded eyes. Where was all the criticism when President Obama, on his second day in office, had to get help from a lawyer on executive orders that he was signing? Where were all the questions about how awkward and un-presidential he looked? What must our allies be thinking to see Obama displaying a seeming lack of command for the office?

Obama should be subjected to the same criticism that Bush had to deal with. He should be subject to the same kind of scrutiny that any other president has had to endure. Why should there be a different standard for him? The scrutiny of the president is extremely limited because of his liberal policy positions. It is also possible that the media and other guilt-ridden people have a complex about a president who looks different than past presidents. As far as I'm concerned, I could care less what the president looks like!

Because of the extremely fragile topic of race in the United States, the notion that Mr. Obama should get a pass because of his skin color is troubling at best. It is akin to anyone trying to tell me that all the sacrifices made by so many people to promote the cause of freedom and liberty for all people in America was in vain. The rulebook for how President Obama is treated should be equal to that of anyone else. The election of Obama ought to be a historical turning point for good in the history of the country if both he and everyone else will allow it. Personally, I believe our country has made progress concerning race and equality long before the election of Barack Obama; in spite of those who seem to want to maintain tension between various ethnic groups.

I am not prone to quoting Juan Williams to support a position, but in this case I believe he says it quite well: "If his presidency is to represent the full power of the idea that black Americans are just like everyone else—fully human and fully capable of intellect, courage, and patriotism—then Barack Obama has to be subject to the same rough and tumble of political criticism experienced by his predecessors. To treat the first black president as if he is a fragile flower is certain to hobble him. It is also to waste a tremendous opportunity for improving race relations by doing away with stereotypes and seeing the potential in all Americans."[76] The mainstream media and everyone else have now received the facts from an award winning journalist and the train is leaving the station. I believe it is time for all the naysayers to get on board and stop stirring the pot of contention when it comes to racism; especially in cases where none exists, as in the Harvard University professor incident.

Mr. Williams went on to say that, "Several seasons ago, when Philadelphia Eagle's black quarterback Donovan McNabb was struggling, radio commentator Rush Limbaugh said the media wanted a black quarterback to do well and gave Mr. McNabb 'a lot of credit for the performance of this team that he didn't deserve.' Mr. Limbaugh's sin was saying out loud what others had said privately. There is a lot more at stake now, and to allow criticism of Mr. Obama only behind closed doors does no honor to the dreams and prayers of generations past: that race be put aside, and all people be judged honestly, openly, and on the basis of their performance. President Obama deserves no less."[77]

It seems to me that among the many issues that prompted the Civil Rights movement was the fact that "blacks" in America were not being treated equal to their "white" brothers. They simply wanted to be given equal access to what was rightfully theirs to pursue, namely "life, liberty, and the pursuit of happiness." Since equal treatment under the law had been denied to "blacks" for so long, the struggle to overcome hate and bigotry in order that these basic rights were finally honored came with a heavy price. As Americans, we can never forget the sacrifices that have been made or the efforts of many to ensure that true freedom and liberty be granted to all citizens. After all, freedom was not bestowed to us by the creation of the Constitution; it is the gift of God, supported by the Constitution, though it was denied for generations because of the wickedness of men.

I submit that the best thing for all Americans to do is to treat people the way they would want others to treat their own children. Neither you nor I can do anything to right the wrongs of the past; we can only do our part to ensure that the hatred of racism is never permitted to worm its way into mainstream America ever again. In the end, I believe God expects us to do all that is within our power to promote equality and liberty for all people. Every individual has to make an effort to accept the fact that we are a collection of human beings, not a collection of different colored human beings. So long as people continue speaking out about how seemingly important our differences are, our obvious differences will remain the focus of who we are, as opposed to our potential to become more unified based on more substantive matters such as character.

My contention is that the differences with regard to skin color should have no bearing on how we treat one another. People who are in a position to speak out about the issues, who can positively impact the dialogue and influence the way we think, need to have the courage to speak up, even if it means stepping out of their comfort zone. I submit, however, that the following is not the way to rise up from the old-school ways of thinking to achieve progress in race relations: "Lord, in the memory of all the saints who from their labors rest, and in the joy of a new beginning, we ask you to help us work for that day when black will not be asked to get in back, when brown can stick around, when yellow will be mellow, when the red man can get ahead, man; and when white will embrace what is right."[78]

If you are not already aware of the previous quote, it is a portion of a prayer delivered by the Reverend Dr. Joseph Lowery, during the benediction at the Inauguration of Barack Obama, forty-fourth President of the United States in 2009! Not 1959! People like Dr. Lowery sacrifice credibility when they stoop to making statements like this, especially when it is part of a prayer to God, no less. I acknowledge that Dr. Lowery seemed to be imploring deity for "the joy of a new beginning," and had he concluded with that, it would most likely have endeared many people to him, including me. However, he did not stop there. For instance, though he may have been subject to sitting in the back of the bus at one time in his life—assuming his reference to "black will not be asked to get in back" is indeed a reference to an ugly time in American history that was beyond despicable; for him to make such an accusatory and unproductive statement in twenty-first century America is irresponsible.

Just like hateful language used by bigoted organizations such as the KKK, Skinheads, and Aryan Nation; the only thing that will be accomplished using divisive language is the further widening of divisions that already exists among some people in this country. I do not see how divisive language, no matter where it comes from, can be viewed as helpful or meaningful to unite Americans. I guess we have been reduced to listening to platitudes and trite statements when it comes to race because it seems that there are few people who actually want to do something constructive when it comes to improving what they often speak about needing improvement.

I do not believe that Dr. Lowery is going to motivate anyone to sit down and discuss improving race relations by choosing to include the kind of rhetoric he used on Inauguration Day. Besides, it takes more than a few people getting together to discuss improving relationships between people before things actually get better. It takes the willingness of those same people to go out into the communities of America to spread the word, as many have demonstrated over the years. It seems like the only time people talk about race relations is when there is a problem or even a perceived problem, and that usually never accomplishes very much. Naturally, in Dr. Lowery's case, the mainstream media gave him a pass and as far as I know have not devoted any attention to this incident that it still deserves.

I would never judge the intent or sincerity of someone else's prayers; however, in this case it seemed as though Dr. Lowery was making a mockery of something that millions of Americans embrace as very important in their daily lives. Furthermore, it is evident that we are left to question the sincerity of those who proclaim unification and equality on the one hand; but by their very words, whether intentionally or not, end up accomplishing the exact opposite. We have come to expect divisive rhetoric from groups like the KKK, because that is what they do, in fact, we would be shocked to hear them proclaim anything different. The Reverend Lowery's words, however, no matter how well intentioned, serve only to sow the seeds of doubt, insincerity and suspicion in the often delicate topic of civil rights in the twenty-first century.

Assessing Dr. Lowery's sincerity, or lack thereof, relating to his choice of words during a benediction, seem to highlight his apparent skin color hang-ups and would hardly seem as a clarion call for people to want to improve race relations. Imagine someone with skin color different from Dr. Lowery's, offering a similarly judgmental prayer. Would I be mistaken if I said that it seems as though there are some in America unwilling to let go of the business of racial divisiveness? It is a given that "hate groups" in America will continue to do what they do, but anyone who really cares and has access to a pulpit, who can make a difference by the way they lead, should do more to unify Americans by using words that motivate people to actually unite.

I realize that everyone is entitled to their opinion, including me, and that means that anyone should be able to state their opinion about something without being characterized as evil. I am reminded of a prominent political couple in America that I credit for having coined a clever little slogan back in the 1990s that went something like: "The politics of personal destruction." The Clintons certainly used it to perfection to deflect attention from more weighty matters. In politics, we all know of those who have come up with nice little sound bites that often tug at the emotions of people, helping to portray that individual as a victim. This type of offensive usually works very well for those who employ it, and often their supporters continue to sympathize with them even if the facts say otherwise.

Dr. Lowery may have received immediate endearment from a small minority of people with the closing words of his benediction on Inauguration Day. However, I suspect that whatever endearing qualities may still exist, they are probably from the knee-jerk types who often fail to exert the kind of mental calisthenics necessary and who probably consider TV shows like Jerry Springer's as substantive. Many of us recognized the kind of language that Dr. Lowery used as nothing more than cute little catchphrases that were anything but substantive.

I wonder if very many of Dr. Lowery's contemporaries who were involved in the civil rights movement honestly agree with the Reverend's method of piety. I believe that Dr. Lowery used the national spotlight for something far less than what he could have, and it seems that instead of devoting time to some coy little phrases, he could have petitioned God with a heartfelt plea for all of His children to unite and be as one. It seems to me that for those who believe racism to be a problem in America, and who are serious about its demise, ought to be willing to tear down any of the remaining walls that may still be standing because of it.

When anyone uses divisive language, whether subtly or otherwise, it shows the inappropriateness that well-intentioned individuals sometimes display. I want to underscore the fact that we are no longer living at a time when someone like Dr. Lowery came of age, for instance. I realize that Dr. Lowery was involved in the struggle for equality in a way that I will never be able to comprehend, and for that, he has my respect. But his is exactly the kind of old-school thinking that must be put on the shelf when it comes to recognizing the progress that America has made for equality; in large measure thanks to many who will probably forever remain nameless, but who, nevertheless were dedicated to the principle that "all men are created equal" and were willing to pay the ultimate price so others might have the kinds of opportunities previous generations had only dreamed about. If there are people who harbor the type of sentiment expressed in Dr. Lowery's prayer, we have a lot of work to do in reconciling a bigoted past and moving forward.

In spite of all that has been said in the past, I do not believe that things in America are as bad as some like to believe. I do not care what anyone says to my face, in a book, on the internet, in the paper, on TV, or anywhere about what they intend to do to rid our society of racism. The only way it can be credible is if their actions support their rhetoric. Those concerned about promoting racial equality must be as vigilant as the hate groups are in disseminating their propaganda relative to racial superiority. And make no mistake about it, hate groups come in all shapes, sizes, and colors. It would seem that Dr. Lowery has damaged his credibility among those interested in promoting equality for all Americans. It is unfortunate, because I am convinced that he has done much to advance the cause of equality throughout his life, but there can be little hope for growth in continuing to classify each other using skin color as a substantive foundation.

It is sad to see a political party that has embraced policies which, in many ways, can only keep America on the path of disunity, class warfare and dependence upon government. The policy platform of democrats and liberalism is not the way to keep America great. The Republican Party, specifically, conservatives often seem like they are not doing a whole lot to actively position themselves to include as many people as possible under the tent of conservatism. The conservative focus should be upon getting as many eligible voters as possible to sincerely change their hearts and minds, to recognize the values of conservatism for all people.

The conservative movement is large enough to accommodate all who are willing to educate themselves, which means paying less attention to mainstream media elites, among other things. An effort has to be made on every level to begin educating all people to support the conservative movement that is presently advocated most often within the GOP. The liberal experiment has done very little, if anything at all, to improve the social or economic conditions of anyone in this country because of its tendency to use taxpayer dollars to do for people what they can, and should do for themselves.

Liberals often embrace such causes as: race based policies that fail to emphasize merit and effort; abortion (once veiled as a woman's right to choose; but now cleverly coined as women's reproductive health issues), constant bemoaning of the gap between the rich and poor (class warfare), and a supposed lack of opportunity for continuing education. I have previously stated, for instance that I believe that it makes no sense to continue clinging to incorrect attitudes about race just because that is the kind of thinking we inherited from a previous generation.

A prominent citizen of the US once said that he hoped that one day his children and others like them would be afforded the right to be judged "by the content of their character," not by the color of their skin. Observe America today and you will see a country that has achieved noteworthy accomplishments with regard to the equal treatment of all people. Of course, we may not be where we want to be collectively, but no one can deny the incredible progress that has been made in a relatively short period of time; all because of a Declaration of Independence and Constitution that support the God given idea for achieving equality.

A lot of liberals admit that there is still a need to give particular groups of people preferential treatment in America; such as those championed by affirmative action. I do not think it is right that one class of people should be entitled to what amounts to government sponsored promotion of a particular class of people over another. Certainly, government influenced by good people was needed in rectifying constitutionally protected rights that should have never been denied in the first place. However, that does not justify government today actively promoting the pursuit of "life, liberty, and happiness" for one class of people at the expense of any other.

There was a time when our government looked the other way in matters of equality by permitting discrimination against people whose skin color was different. Sadly, there is nothing you or I can do now to rectify something so unacceptable and heinous that happened in our history. However, there is plenty we can do to make sure that it is never allowed to occur again; to any race, male or female. We cannot allow the kind of behavior that creates an unfair advantage or keeps people down to be acceptable. We cannot justify the past with equally damning behavior going forward. It has been said that "Affirmative action creates a constitutional paradox. You do something unequal to create equality eventually. The Constitution says we must treat all people equally, but affirmative action treats some people unequally, actually more equally. This creates constitutional tension."[79] Affirmative action is a classic example of a law being created, whose unintended consequence has usurped the rights contained in the Constitution relative to equality.

People often speak of equal opportunity. What is equal opportunity? Simply put, it is equal access. I often view sports as a way to better understand various aspects of human relations. In the world of sports, let's take the National Basketball Association (NBA) for instance; most of us could agree that there are varying degrees of talent that make up the pool of potential NBA players, taken from the ranks of the college players, various developmental leagues, and overseas leagues—both professional and otherwise. There are thirty NBA teams with twelve players per team, for a total of 360 players in the entire NBA. Anyone who follows the NBA will tell you that the talent level is diverse. This diversity of talent means that every player is paid a salary equal to his abilities and talents because teams exist to make money, not unlike any other profit-making venture. For instance, everyone knows that LeBron James commands a much greater salary than, say, Adam Morrison. Does that make Mr. Morrison unequal to Mr. James? It would seem so. Does it mean that it is unfair? No. Again, NBA teams are businesses, and like all businesses in a capitalistic society, they exist to minimize loss and maximize profits. Should the NBA begin dictating to the owners of their respective teams that they pay each player an equal sum regardless of their level of talent? If that were to be the case, LeBron James would have an exceedingly legitimate argument to support his claims of being cruelly underpaid.

What about all the guys that do not make it to the NBA? Should something be done so that they, too, could be entitled to the opportunity of playing in the NBA? Should the government step in and mandate that certain quotas be followed? Should affirmative action procedures be taken into consideration to give those who are considered "minorities" the opportunity to play in the NBA? Well, no need to worry about this and other possible scenarios, because something has been done to make the process as fair and equitable as it can be. And for the last fifty or sixty years, it seems to have been working just fine: it's called the free market—not some governmental bureaucratically created arm designed to make things "fair."

Because of the free market, various developmental leagues have been formed with the objective to get a player to the next level if that is his desire. There has also been an explosion of leagues in Europe and elsewhere that are designed to prepare potential NBA talent. Even China has gotten in on the act! The simple truth is that every young man that has the talent to play in the NBA has an equal opportunity to do so. If you happen to be good enough, work hard, and maybe have some luck on your side, perhaps you too can play in the NBA. If not, then you just might have to live out your dream in one of the other leagues or maybe even find your dream elsewhere.

We all know that success in the NBA does not come on talent alone, regardless of how talented a player may have been in any other league. Ultimately, to be a player in the NBA, your skin color is insignificant, whether you have hair or not won't matter, whether or not you can make free throws or even if you are not very tall. What does matter for anyone who wants to play in the NBA is that as long as the essential skills are possessed, along with the right work ethic and desire to excel, you might become the next LeBron James. Not likely, but look at it this way, even if you ride the bench, you are still living beyond the dream.

People often talk about the need for diversity in our culture, especially in the workplace. Unfortunately, our society has defined diversity, based in large measure, on skin color. Diversity is "The fact or quality of being diverse: difference." And diverse is, "Unlike in kind: distinct."[80] So even though both LeBron James and Adam Morrison play basketball in the NBA, there is a distinct difference in their abilities to play the game, which difference dictates how much each player will earn throughout the course of his career.

We need to look at the diversity of talent in the NBA, not the diversity of talent based on skin tone. If we focused on color, then I imagine that people who are not perhaps "black" might have a legitimate complaint, since it is a known fact that a majority of players in the NBA have skin that has darker pigmentation. When I sit down to watch an NBA game, I want to be entertained by the best possible talent, not to mention referees who can actually call a traveling violation. If we were going to use fairness as a measurement, then anyone with sub-mediocre abilities should be allowed to play in the NBA regardless of color or gender, because that's "fair."

I understand that human beings can be extremely superficial and that my NBA analogy is not necessarily emblematic of our workforce generally. I understand that sometimes people are passed over for a job because the person responsible for hiring sometimes makes a decision based upon physical characteristics about a particular individual, bias against another person because of learned behavior that is incorrect or a host of other issues besides merit.

Human beings tend to rate other human beings based upon physical appearance: too short, too fat, too skinny, too tall, too "black," too "white;" and we cannot forget—too ugly. Most of us are aware of the efforts that supporters of affirmative action have taken to "level" the playing field for "blacks," but I want to know what those same supporters have done for anyone not currently playing in the NBA that wants to, regardless of skin color; because after all, I thought affirmative action was all about access for minorities.

What about every other sport or industry? Is it fair to have an organization promote one class of people while discriminating against every other? Unfortunately, affirmative action is most often applied to a very narrow set of standards, it is akin to a woman saying that she is a "little" pregnant. You cannot have it both ways, you are either for the advancement of all humans collectively, ensuring equal access to the process, or you are not. We live at a time when we should be satisfied with the most qualified person getting the job because they took the time and made the effort to move ahead on their own accord instead of relying on the government or someone else to do it for them. Unfortunately, as was pointed out earlier, a man like Clarence Thomas will always retain in the back of his mind that he was judged by the color of his skin rather than by the content of his character or the brilliance of his intellect.

As far as I am aware, you can be any color you want and still gain access to all the formal education that you could possibly need or have the inclination to obtain, for that matter. What sort of legacy do we want to pass to our children? Have the standards for public education been so diminished by the very people who claim to support it? Well, I do not know the answer to these questions. What I do know is that like many things in our society, personal responsibility has all but been removed from the equation whenever those concerned about education talk about its failures. I suggest that rather than the education system failing us; in many instances, we have failed in the education of our children and we often want someone else to fix it for us, like depending on government to do so.

I would submit that if parents, legal guardians, extended family and those concerned about the success of their children's education; become active and remain so by holding educator's responsible for what is going on in the classroom. In many ways we have allowed children to dictate their educational progress instead of adults holding children responsible. Education is so much more than what goes on behind the doors of a classroom. It takes those of us who are concerned about it taking the time necessary to inspire our young people to crave learning like they might crave pizza, video games or texting. Education does not happen by accident, it requires the right mindset and environment to prepare young people for the real world and how to treat and deal with others respectfully, thus preparing them to seek gainful employment and a lifetime of self-reliance and productivity, not to mention the need for continuous education beyond the formal. The bottom line is that educational assistance is available to anyone in 21st Century America that is willing to work and sacrifice to obtain it.

I am saddened by people who have the mistaken belief that the responsibility for their education or their children's education rests with someone else, rather than with the person in the mirror. The lack of opportunity for a good education is one thing that some in this country continue to try and exploit for their own pitiful self-interests. For instance, how long has the government been pumping money into the public school system on the one hand, while on the other, practically all politicians complain every election cycle about how horrible the education system is and how they pledge to do something about it? Clearly, more money is not the answer to public school system woes as presently constituted. There must be a different set of incentives to attract would-be teachers to pursue teaching as a career.

Credible people must admit the sad truth about public education, which is that it will not get better until attitudes are changed regarding the responsibility for education in the first place. At least a few things need to take place in order for public education to improve in this country: First, government must limit its involvement in public education unless it intends to perpetually satisfy the status quo. Second, the issue of union control as well as tenured teacher incompetence and complacency must be addressed. And third, perhaps education in this country should begin to move to the private sector, where compensation for teachers would surely increase because of market competition.

I refuse to accept the notion that those who lament about their limited opportunities for obtaining a good education is due to their belonging to a "minority" group. Every citizen is supposed to be personally responsible and is obliged to seek the best education possible as long as they are mentally capable, that is why it is so important for parents and others to be responsible for their children and provide the best foundation possible for their children to be able to learn. However, it seems that in our society today, too many parents have shifted the responsibility of educating their children to someone else, usually the state. And naturally, bureaucrats are more than willing to continue screwing things up and satisfying themselves at the ballot box. But this is the United States of America, opportunities abound when it comes to education!

If an individual has the willingness to work and make the necessary sacrifices to get a good education, there is no limit to the amount of formal or informal education one can receive. As a matter of fact, one of the best places to begin is for parents and guardian's to be their kid's parent and stop trying to be their best friend. Establish some rules, like insisting that their children stop watching so much television, playing video games, and doing a host of other useless and wasteful activities. It is practically criminal when considering how much of our tax dollars have been wasted on lazy, apathetic, yet capable people. The problem among many in our society is that there seems to be a lack of effort to be better educated and improve personal circumstances. I have little sympathy for those who claim to have little opportunity but make no effort to change.

Our formal education is ultimately outweighed by the education that we get through a lifetime of investigation, inquiry, reading, pondering, and studying; in other words, applying ourselves. However, I cannot stress the importance of receiving formal education beyond High School in order to enhance the employment opportunities afterword. Personally, I did not realize the value of my own formal education until well into adulthood. And the reason for that rests squarely with me, in spite of the efforts of others or even the lack thereof. I know many professionals in a variety of fields and they may never know the profound respect I have for them because they understood the importance of committing to their personal formal education. They had a vision of where they wanted to be and they worked tirelessly to get to that point.

It takes very little effort to observe people who would rather complain about their lack of opportunity instead of determining that nothing will stop them from getting the kind of education they want for themselves and their children. Personally, though my father talked about the importance of college; neither he nor my mother emphasized the importance of discovering the kind of career choices I could have made, using education as the impetus. But I do not blame them for my not knowing what I wanted to do or not having graduated from college until later in life. Regardless of what I may think about what my parents did or did not do relative to my education, ultimately I had to take responsibility for my own education.

Blaming parents, the school, teachers, government, or whomever is a copout and a complete waste of time and effort. If someone wants to get an education in this country, do the things that are necessary to make it happen, have the guts to stand up to others who may think you are being a "sellout" when it comes to education; there is no shame in overcoming ignorance, only remorse if you do not do what it takes to educate yourself. If someone in your immediate or extended family, peers, or even your culture is not supportive or is even dismissive of your efforts to get all the education you can—reject such attitudes as nonsense and start knocking down the obstacles that stand in your way instead of seeing them as impenetrable barriers.

I want to briefly discuss a liberal policy that has done irreparable damage to society. It is a well known fact that, generally speaking democrats have embraced abortion as a platform issue even though they often tip-toe around it at election time. Abortion seems to arouse the deepest emotions in people. I am against abortion unless the health of the mother is at stake. Obviously, in cases of rape or incest, very personal decisions must be made and no one should condemn the choice made by those who have been traumatized, no matter what. In other instances where an abortion might be performed, it ought to be handled on a case-by-case circumstance based upon a given set of facts. But in situations where life can be protected, all things being equal, I believe every measure should be taken to do so.

Perhaps instead of putting so much emphasis on whether or not a woman should get an abortion in cases where none of the three circumstances mentioned previously is present; more emphasis ought to be placed on personal responsibility. Adoption is a great way of providing a child to a couple not able to have children on their own. Many such organizations are available to facilitate such a choice. Also, in many cases children slip through the cracks and end up in foster care and may never be adopted, crossing the threshold into adulthood on potentially unstable social ground. This takes us back to the issue of personal choices. Responsibility for bringing another human being into the world is enormous and can often have detrimental consequences.

Abortion always seems to center on the decision of a woman's choice as opposed to whether a man has rights in the decision. In this case, I am speaking of scenarios not involving the mother's health, rape, or incest. I could care less about what the courts have ruled when it comes to the rights of males in abortion cases involving committed relationships. As long as there is no abuse, the father should have some rights when it comes to deciding whether to keep the child or not.

I believe that all men (and young men) not involved in a committed (marriage) relationship, who father a child are in danger of having their rights ignored when it comes to abortion. In other words, the mother of the child deserves all the rights to carry the child to term, and either giving the child up for adoption or making the choice to keep the baby. To me, the option to abort is taken off the table once the decision is made to have sexual intercourse, all things being equal. Conception is the ultimate moment for any man to prove his manhood and support his act of passion by taking upon himself the responsibility of being a dad, which is much different than simply being able to father a child.

I suppose that liberals and those who support abortion will ever cling to it as a personal choice without any regard for the rights of a fetus to be permitted the experience of mortality and ultimately become what all liberals love: a tax payer! It is time for the issue of abortion to be put into the hands of the several states and out of the hands of the federal government.

ROLE, PURPOSE, AND POWER OF GOVERNMENT

Following is a pertinent question to ask ourselves these days—what has happened concerning the evolution of our government? In many respects, we have digressed to a level well below the aspirations that the founding fathers must have had for this nation. But as discussed in the previous chapter, we have actually progressed as a nation that recognizes that all human beings, not just Americans, have certain "inalienable rights," which makes the Declaration of Independence truly remarkable to everyone blessed by its language. The concept of freedom and independence is a fact in America today, whereas at the time the Declaration of Independence was ratified, it was only recognized theoretically for some people for many generations until finally becoming a reality for all people in America.

That reality has far and away eclipsed what the founders did not conceive about true equality at the time. A wise proverb states that, "Where there is no vision, the people perish: but he that keepeth the law, happy is he."[81] Reasonably thinking people cannot deny America's vision or the fact that this is a country that has been emulated by other nations, but its Constitution has never been duplicated. The vision of liberty is one that most freedom-loving people desire across the world. Like the abolition of slavery, America tends to lead the way with respect to matters of great human significance. Perhaps an area that we are trying to find our way is in regard to determining the role, purpose, and power of elected politicians in the evolution of our government today.

The founders of our nation were inspired to establish the groundwork for how the elected stewards of our nation, at any time, govern. With the establishment of the legislative branch of the government, a mechanism became operative whereby laws could be created by which, at least in theory, the Constitution would be upheld. Since laws are the foundation for maintaining a civilized society, and given the relatively few times the United States Constitution has been amended; this speaks volumes about the bedrock foundation upon which this nation was established.

In addition to the legislative branch, the founding fathers created the judicial and executive branches of government. The establishment of co-equal branches of government created what we have come to know as a means of checks and balances. In theory, no single branch of government should ever be able to enact complete dominance over another, or over the people for that matter. And by the same token, we must insure that no individual ever has absolute power within our form of government, in spite of how much the people may be mesmerized by the charisma of their elected leaders.

Our judicial branch is charged with the authority to interpret law and make accurate, unbiased rulings based solely upon the facts, and nothing else. I realize that precedent plays a significant role which the courts take into consideration when making rulings, however, it would seem to reason that if a particular precedent were incorrect, that an outcome based in part on such a precedent, may be equally incorrect or wrong as well. At no time could the founding fathers have envisioned members of the judiciary who have such a lust for making law simply because their fingers wrap around a gavel.

The executive branch has a specific duty, among other things, to protect the people as the Commander in Chief over military forces, the right to veto legislation or sign it into law and appoint judges. The president is not a legislator. The system by which we are governed is an ingenious structure, but not perfect. Unfortunately, like a lot of things, man has found a way to corrupt our system. The seeds of this corruption are many, namely: power, money, control, and dominance.

I believe most of us would agree that the system of government that we have in the United States is the envy of many a third world country. If you do not agree, try living in North Korea, Cuba, Somalia, Iran, or a host of other nations where all the liberties we enjoy here in America are scarce or nonexistent. We tend to take our freedom for granted because we are so accustomed to the kind of lifestyle we live from one day to the next. There are even a host of western nations that I would not mind visiting, but forget about living in any of them for the rest of my life, not because it wouldn't be a good experience; but for the sake of argument let's just say that I am partial to the United States. I believe we are truly a blessed people, and that we must continually strive to be worthy, as a free people, to merit the blessings of divine providence.

By default, when some of our peers receive the political endorsement of the people, they inherit a measure of power so long as they occupy a particular office. Oftentimes, it seems that the people are willing to continue voting for many of these career power seekers until they become firmly entrenched. And it seems that the longer one can occupy an office, the more power he not only often obtains, but also that he usually sees himself as actually being more powerful. That is scary! For this reason term limits should become a reality. Because of the corruptible nature of man, it makes sense to have term limits on the legislative and judicial branches of government to ensure that no one is able to establish themselves as a permanent fixture in the halls of Congress or in the courts, which can often lead to the attitude that the individual is more important than the people.

I realize that this is nothing new, and that there are those who argue that term limits only mean that new people have to learn the legislative process, for instance, which slows down an already intentionally deliberate process. But what better way to keep the legislative process at least somewhat honest. And it would force the lobbyists to be more creative, which may not be a good thing for them. But why not limit members of Congress to twelve years and judges to a similar term? Something must be done to limit the potential for corruption that seems to often get worse with seniority. Again, part of the problem in government today is that the power brokers who run the show are so adept at overcomplicating legislation with a load of hot air and special interest earmarks that the rest of us often get the shaft. And sometimes we become apathetic or indifferent to it all. Sadly, that is exactly how some who have the power want to keep it. They must figure that the more we are dissatisfied with the process, the better it is for them.

I believe term limits might be the answer, to keep rascals in check, even if that means we have to endure them through the full length of a single term. Perhaps you may be thinking that if term limits were the answer, how come the founding fathers failed to make clear provisions for it in the Constitution? I suppose the obvious answer is that they probably could not have anticipated the lust for power that many in our day literally seem to crave. Furthermore, with respect to the judiciary, I am certain that the founding fathers had no way of anticipating judges who would one day try to make laws perched high atop their benches, or collectively seek to overturn the voice of the people, as demonstrated by the California State Supreme Court's decision to ignore the will of the people with respect to the definition of marriage—thus necessitating the need for Proposition 8 to be on the ballot in the state recently.

But this is the kind of thing we have to deal with today; out of control legislators and judges who have had help becoming corrupted by the fringe minority that collectively seem to yearn for the power to control things the way they want, without regard for the voice of the majority of the people. Finally, it is nice to know that the twenty-second amendment to the Constitution takes care of term limiting the executive branch. All of these issues, and many others, demonstrate the importance of the Constitution in a civilized society.

It is necessary to point out some examples regarding why all three branches of our government need term limits. Within his first month in office, President Obama signed an executive order that he believed would "level the playing field"[82] between labor unions and management. The president appointed Vice President Joe Biden as the chairman of a newly formed "task force on the problems of middle-class Americans."[83] Great, all we needed was another "task force" to further clog the system with superfluous bureaucratic babble; not that the vice president is so busy in the first place, but in the case of Joe Biden, less is more. The president further stated that, "We need to level the playing field for workers and the unions that represent their interests ... I do not view the labor movement as part of the problem. To me, it's part of the solution ... You cannot have a strong middle class without a strong labor movement."[84] What? I would say that we cannot have a strong "labor movement" without a strong employer movement. What the president should concentrate on is leading the charge for Congress to lighten the tax burden so that companies will have the means to reinvest in their businesses through innovation, research, and development.

I wonder if the president realizes why so many companies manufacture and produce overseas. There are obviously many reasons why American companies have made the choice to operate overseas, such as a cheap labor force or not having to be responsible for paying health premiums of its employee's; which, since mandated health care coverage has become the law of the land here, the burden's on employer's and employee's will become even heavier because of an even more stringent and increased tax liability to pay for such enormous spending. And it will only get worse if more of Obama's philosophies relative to tax policy become reality. It is amazing that businesses can still be profitable in America today, which says a lot about the ingenuity of American businesses. So if the Obama administration wants to do something to fix the tax and regulation burdens that have been placed upon the backs of American ingenuity; take it from an average citizen, lighten the tax burdens, and we will see an improvement in the "labor movement," otherwise jobs will continue to disappear.

Let me continue by quoting from none other than James Hoffa, who just happened to be present at the signing of the so called middle-class executive order. He said that "It's a new day for workers ... We finally have a White House that is dedicated to working with us to rebuild our middle class. Hope for the American Dream is being restored."[85] Yes, thankfully the executive branch is term limited so that this kind of idiotic thinking is curtailed from seeing the light of day. Now all we need is a time machine, because I don't think anyone would argue against the need for labor to be unified and organized; the impact of organized labor had great benefits in ensuring that individuals in the workforce received the kind of protection needed from abusive companies throughout our history. However, we are no longer living during the nineteenth or twentieth centuries. Please do not get me wrong, there was a time when unions were essential in helping to protect the safety and well-being of workers. It would seem that we are no longer living under the kind of deplorable conditions today that existed generations ago, and which made unions obligatory to protect workers.

A simple observation of the automotive unions and their crippling effect on the "big three" automakers in the US will probably lend credence to how unions have seemingly outlived their usefulness. Naturally, the leaders of the automotive union would never admit that they are essentially biting the hand that feeds them; however, in private, the answer would probably produce something closer to the truth. Perhaps the reason why foreign automakers have been able to dominate American automakers is due to the fact that the "big three" have had to cut costs in manufacturing to keep up with the demands of the union for current workers and maintaining retirement packages for retirees.

Unions have probably made unreasonable demands over the years regarding health care and pensions, for example, just because they could. The "big three" have capitulated to a point of seeming no return. I recognize that there are those who are on the opposite side of viewpoints I have just expressed; but that is the beauty of America, we have the right to disagree. I am also aware that in order to recover from a serious downturn, recognition of problems need to be acknowledged and necessary action taken to correct them. I have had my share of blue collar jobs over the years, and even joined the effort to form a union at one point during one of those jobs, so I appreciate the right to unionize. Having said that, I do not believe it to be in the best interest of the people for government to take over private enterprise or exercise usurpation in such affairs as with

185

the government's role in something like the CEO of GM, Rick Waggoner's "stepping down," if that's what you call it.

Naturally, President Obama is going to do everything possible, even if it's only perception, to rescue the poor, not just the middle class. He said: "We're not forgetting the poor. They are going to be front and center, because they, too, share our American Dream ... if they're willing to work for it."[86] I am hesitant to ask what the president's idea of work might be, but I bet most people can usually feel the grip around their wallet tightening when they hear the president say that, "We're not forgetting the poor." It may sound as if I have something against people who work for a living; I do not. I have spent the better part of my working life counted among the "working class." I have had jobs in my adult life when I only made a few thousand dollars a year, but regardless of what we work for, we ought to be counted among the "working class." The point I am making here is that I do not care if you are educated or not; blue collar or white; work with your hands or your head; if you work for it, you are part of the "working class." Obviously, some people may sweat a lot more than others or get really dirty while earning their income, some wear jeans and boots, some neckties or dresses, while still others wear a uniform. Regardless, I guess the beauty of America is that everyone is free to choose what line of work he or she will do, and it should not necessarily be up to the government to mandate or control.

The duly appointed chairman of the task force to deal with "problems of middle-class" Americans, Vice President Biden had this to say about the newly organized governmentally controlled task force: "With this task force, we have a single, highly visible group with one single goal: to raise the living standards of the people who are the backbone of this country."[87] Since when has any governmental bureaucrat done anything to "raise the living standards" of anyone in this country? Where is the transparency so that we can know the progress of the "task force" and make sure it is achieving its aims to raise "the living standards of the people who are the backbone of this country?" Sadly, the transparency that we were promised by this administration seems to only exist in the minds of those who are members of it.

The reality about the Obama administration and a democrat controlled congress is that taxes are going to be raised unless they have a sudden epiphany. And whenever taxes are raised, the living standards of people who actually pay taxes in this country go down. Whenever welfare programs are allowed to be abused, the living standards and dignity of people in this country go down. Whenever our government gets bigger and more intrusive into the lives of the people, the living standards, creativity and entrepreneurial spirit of people in this country is always diminished.

I have nothing against those who make very little money, but it seems to me that the backbone of this country is the innovators, the entrepreneurs, people who create the jobs that allow the citizens of this country to acquire and maintain a standard of living that is unparalleled in the world. Our high living standards allow you and me to pay for a home, an automobile, and even some of the finer things in life that are available to those who put forth the effort and work using their God-given abilities. Of course, there is a mutually beneficial association between those who provide the labor and those who perform the labor. But even the poor in this country have it better off than most people throughout the earth, especially those living in the third world.

Our government is not, nor should it ever be, in the business of creating jobs that will provide its citizens with the things that I have mentioned, and more. Our government should not be in the business of stifling the growth and potential of its citizens (regardless of their economic status) with the burdens that it so willingly places on the backs of those who have the determination and the guts to take the risks necessary, which ultimately benefit all who work. I do not believe that a majority of Americans agree with the redistribution of wealth to the extent that some liberals, including Obama, want to take it.

Following is the kind of leadership that is very much needed, and which seems to be completely absent in politics today: "In this present crisis, government is not the solution to our problem; government is the problem. From time to time we've been tempted to believe that society has become too complex to be managed by self-rule, that government by an elite group is superior to government for, by, and of the people. Well, if no one among us is capable of governing himself, then who among us has the capacity to govern someone else? All of us together, in and out of government, must bear the burden. The solutions we seek must be equitable, with no one group singled out to pay a higher price."[88]

Is there anyone in government today that has the guts, like Ronald Reagan, to speak the truth about how government is to blame for many of the woes that we now lament? The fire and passion with which Reagan so eloquently spoke is seemingly absent among conservatives today. It seems that too many people today want to burden government with those things that individuals can and should do for themselves. In many ways, we have become a nation of dependents. All one need do is to remember the health care debate to see the impact of where we are with regard to the entitlement mentality.

We can be confident that the kind of wisdom we need will be found in this statement by Reagan, which needs to be understood by the mainstream:

> "We hear much of special interest groups. Well, our concern must be for a special interest group that has been too long neglected. It knows no sectional boundaries or ethnic and racial divisions, and it crosses political lines. It is made up of men and women who raise our food, patrol our streets, man our mines and factories, teach our children, keep our homes, and heal us when we're sick—professionals, industrialists, shopkeepers, clerks, cabbies, and truck drivers. They are, in

short, 'we the people,' this breed called Americans ... We are a nation that has a government—not the other way around. And this makes us special among the nations of the earth. Our government has no power except that granted it by the people. It is time to check and reverse the growth of government, which shows signs of having grown beyond the consent of the governed ... Now, so there will be no misunderstanding, it's not my intention to do away with government. It is rather to make it work—work with us, not over us; to stand by our side, not ride on our back. Government can and must provide opportunity, not smother it; foster productivity, not stifle it"[89]

Reagan clearly believed that government has its place; that it should never act as an entity with the ability to be completely dominant in the lives of the people. I believe that if he were around today, Reagan would be appalled at what has become of the scope and size of government. Not only that, but I believe he would be shocked to see the lack of industry, both in the manufacture of goods as well as the degradation of character among those in Washington, in particular. There is no reason that we should be saddled with a tax burden on business that is one of the highest in the world; and further, that those in government have the audacity to be critical of businesses that make the difficult choice to set up shop outside the country. It is one thing to unwittingly enact tax laws that ultimately and inevitably grow the size of government, but quite another to knowingly place tax burdens upon the people, furthering the reality of less productivity and even greater job losses, which burden the "poor" more than others. The way out of an economic mess is not to have government loosen the reins of spending, but to actually tighten the hold on those reins to manage spending that is out of control.

I do not have the ability to stress adequately the significance of the fact that I have spent, not only the bulk of my working life, but the balance of my life to this point, living and being amongst those on the lower rungs of the "labor movement." I have never started a company and I know that I am not alone in that regard. The majority of Americans spend most of their lives working for someone else, which seems to be quite acceptable to most of us. However, it seems to me that liberal politicians often spend too much time maintaining, even creating, conflict between the job creators and the doers of those jobs. Through creativity and ingenuity, anyone in this country is at liberty to start a company, create an invention, or do something to generate an income by using the internet or technology in general. There are numerous ways to lawfully make money in this country, none of which need the sanction or blessing of governmental bureaucrats to succeed. Moreover, I imagine that all of those innovators would like to be left alone so that they can continue to create the jobs and provide the opportunity for the standard of living that so many of us desire, but who may have no inclination to start a business of our own.

Our elected leaders are always whining that there is not enough oversight for this or that. What about oversight for the Congress of the United States? It is quite a scary proposition that the body designated to make laws for the rest of us has such an extremely difficult time policing itself. My guess is that it probably has something to do with power, money, control and dominance. How long are "we the people" going to put up with the way Congress feigns outrage about an issue to which they presume the American people will actually be outraged about? Are we too preoccupied with our own lives that we will remain apathetic or indifferent to the abuse of power that seems to be perpetrated upon us day after day?

For instance, the Speaker of the House, Nancy Pelosi, addressing a throng of reporters about the CIA and "water boarding," said that: "They misled us all the time ... they misrepresented every step of the way, and they don't want that focus on them, so they try to turn the attention on us."[90] The Speaker needs to come clean with the American people. For a another healthy dose of outrage, I recommend a refresher course in the way Congress and the President refused to accept any of the blame for American economic turmoil, and which Mr. Obama compounded by signing into law the biggest spending bill in the history of mankind. All of this on the backs of the "stimulus" bill that Bush signed into law before leaving office. Both bills, we were told, were necessary in order to keep our economy from collapsing. That is outrageous and unacceptable.

Here is another incident that many believe to be outrageous. We all remember the incident involving the Somali pirates that overtook the *Maersk Alabama* in the Indian Ocean in April 2009; and the eventual outcome of that attack, thanks to Navy Seals. We were all elated to know that none of the crew of the *Alabama,* or its captain were severely injured or killed in the attack. However, it is interesting how the media and others decided to react to what happened to the pirates when a liberal is occupying the White House.

Simply stated, elements of the U.S. Military engaged civilians from another country, ultimately ending their lives in a brilliant operation during the cover of darkness, freeing the captain of a civilian merchant ship, who most likely would have been executed had the rescue attempt failed. I have absolutely no problem with any of that. However, I wonder how a largely liberal media would have reacted had someone like George W. Bush still been in the White House and had authorized such an attack. Actually, I have no doubt about how they would have reacted; it would have been so predictable.

Here is where I have a problem with what went down after the rescue of the *Alabama.* Three "black" civilian Somali pirates were killed in the rescue; young men simply looking for a way to survive by doing what they thought they had to do because of otherwise miserable conditions at home. Where was the outcry from all the groups and organizations that would have condemned the attack had a conservative been in the White House? Well, there was none.

Generally, liberals tend to loathe the military when it is tasked by a conservative president to perform a mission like the one in the Indian Ocean that saved American civilian lives. But when a liberal president like Obama gave the order for the military to engage civilian targets from another country, it is something that essentially every liberal manages to overlook, be they part of the media or not. What a double standard! Even Obama's supposed reluctance to use the military, a ruse to convince his liberal friends that he did not actually want to use military force, drew no ire from the media.

Naturally, Bush would have been denounced by people all over the world, not just by the Somali's. The evidence of this for liberals is the Iraq war. It is a double standard that liberals hate to admit, but they know it is true. For instance, they know that Bush was responsible for the surge in Iraq yet they will have no problem giving Obama all the credit for whatever good has come, and will yet come from such a military tactic.

I was under the impression that the Obama administration was going to do away with the partisan rancor that exists in politics. I forgot that campaigning is not like real-life politics; just as I must have forgotten that Pinocchio was a puppet, not a real boy, that is, until the fairy came. The Obama administration needs to reveal the identity of the political fairy!

In all seriousness here is some evidence that clearly demonstrates the lengths that the current administration is willing to go when it comes to defining what they believe their purpose to be. The US Department of Homeland Security published a document dated April 7, 2009, prepared by the *Extremism and Radicalization Branch* of the department. If the report had discussed the kind of extremism demonstrated on September 11, 2001, that would have been fine, but the document was a pathetic piece of propaganda aimed at citizens of the United States, not actual terrorists. It certainly did not take the Obama administration very long to show us their true colors. Everyone that I know who is familiar with the document, plus every intellectually honest person in the media, have denounced the report itself as radical even though it was produced and sanctioned by a president that did not seem to be too bothered by its content. This report is one of the most outrageous documents to come out of any administration in the history of our country. And the contrived apology after the fact means absolutely nothing to me.

First of all, the document is devoid of substantive evidence to support the accusatory and inflammatory language that appears throughout it. Second, it does not matter to me that DHS Secretary Janet Napolitano apologized, after the fact, for the way the report depicts service members who are "returning veterans." For someone who has been the governor of a state and who now serves in the Obama administration, it is shameful, disgraceful, and inexcusable for Ms. Napolitano to condone this: "Returning veterans possess combat skills and experience that are attractive to rightwing extremists. DHS … is concerned that rightwing extremists will attempt to recruit and radicalize returning veterans in order to boost their violent capabilities."[91] Can you imagine the outcry from the media and others if this had been said about the potential of leftwing extremists or any other class of people who may potentially join a radical organization for the purpose of acting out radical violence? Again, this report is beyond shameful and should have never been permitted to be written, let alone disseminated. Ah, yes, hope and change at its best!

I could probably duplicate the whole report in the body of this work, but I will show some restraint, which is more than I can say for DHS under Obama. "Rightwing extremists have capitalized on the election of the first African American president, and are focusing their efforts to recruit new members, mobilize existing supporters, and broaden their scope and appeal through propaganda, but they have not yet turned to attack planning."[92] Are you kidding me? "Attack planning?" They're talking about citizens of the United States who have sacrificed so much to serve the country that they love. See what

I mean about accountability? Unfortunately, nothing will probably ever be done to punish anyone in the administration for producing such a horrible piece of trash!

The whole report on "rightwing extremism" is very troubling in so many ways. As a matter of fact, if you were to take out all the references to anything American, even Dick Durbin would legitimately believe it to be a report prepared by members of the old Soviet Union reminding its citizens of the importance of falling in lockstep with the Communist regime. I am being as serious as I can be, and everyone who reads the report should be equally alarmed. Do you think these people are going to be so blatant as to publish a report like this and pretend that they really did not mean to say the things that they did? If anyone believes such lunacy, I have a condo on Mars that's in a really nice part of the planet, which I am willing to sell at a really good rate.

The current administration is capable of accomplishing their designs by direct means, such as in the DHS report, but don't be fooled by the more subtle means they employ to attempt to accomplish the same objectives, which is to completely dominate the political scene, and punishing those who dissent. I believe that extreme liberals like those who authored this report believe that everyone is supposed to agree with everything they do and say. Look, if they were trying to "test the waters" to see what kind of reaction they would receive, I believe they succeeded. The people in this country who love everything about the Obama administration and who never question anything these people do were not alarmed about the report, and the administration knows it.

> "DHS...assesses that a number of economic and political factors are driving resurgence in rightwing extremist recruitment and radicalization activity. Despite similarities to the climate of the 1990's, the threat posed by lone wolves and small terrorist cells is more pronounced than in past years.

In addition, the historical election of an African American president and the prospect of policy changes are proving to be a driving force for rightwing extremist recruitment and radicalization."[93]

It is absolutely pointless that DHS and the Obama administration made the call that they would no longer refer to the war against terrorists as the "war on terror;" a switch from Bush administration characterization. Fine, but while Obama seems perfectly content to refer to the "war on terror" as a "man caused ... " whatever, it appears that he has no problem referring to American citizens that his administration believes could potentially be threatening to the government, as being a part of "small terrorist cells." What rock did these people crawl out from underneath, that they are so weak that they cannot refer to legitimate forms of terrorism for what it is; because they certainly have no problem accusing fellow American citizens of being "terrorists." It's despicable, sickening, and qualifies as treasonous as far as I'm concerned. Oh no, do I now qualify as a "small terrorist cell" because I think the actions of the Obama administration's DHS is treasonous?

Interestingly, the DHS report sites as an example of their "lone wolves and small terrorist cells," a shooting that took place in Pittsburgh, on April 4, 2009, a mere three days prior to the DHS report surfacing. The report states about the incident in Pittsburgh that: "The alleged gunmen's reaction reportedly was influenced by his racist ideology and belief in antigovernment conspiracy theories related to gun confiscations, citizen detention camps, and a Jewish-controlled one world government."[94] Amazing that the administration was able to glean that kind of information in so short a period of time, when typically the government moves at a much slower pace.

Speaking of periods of time, I do not believe it to be ironic that the administration published their document exactly one week before the historic "Tea Parties" that were to be held all over the country, designed to protest against the administration and Congress for their inability to control spending and tax policy, among other things. It must have been alarming to the administration to know that thousands of people would take to the streets using perfectly legitimate First Amendment rights to protest against an administration anointed to unite us all as one, so long as it is according to their terms. The shooting in Pittsburgh aside, the DHS report is something of a self-fulfilling prophecy. It is spineless and cowardly.

Do some of the items in the following quote sound like something that those participating in the "Tea Parties" might have been protesting: "Many rightwing extremists are antagonistic toward the new presidential administration and its perceived stance on a range of issues, including immigration and citizenship, the expansion of social programs to minorities, and restrictions on firearms ownership and use."[95] Of course, they left out some of the "range of issues" such as "tax and spend" recklessness, the redistribution of the people's money toward those things that they deem worthy, just to name a couple. And what is this business of antagonism toward the administration for "the expansion of social programs to minorities" all about? What on earth could possibly be left to expand with regard to social programs? All of these tactics and many more that we have yet to see are slick tricks to delegitimize legal protests against the government, particularly the Obama administration and its policies.

For the mainstream media and the Obama administration to fail to recognize the "Tea Parties" as an effort by the "silent majority" to voice their opinion about policies to which they do not subscribe; and further, for the media not to give it the coverage it deserves, like they did the immigration rallies, for instance, a few years ago, simply shows the double standard to which the mainstream media is guilty. I believe that we could say with relative certainty that the current government has a greater paranoia and fear of what they think citizens of this country may do, as opposed to the real terrorists who want to destroy our way of life by any means possible. Losing our rights as citizens may appear subtle at first, or perhaps even unbelievable; but all it takes is for law abiding citizens to do nothing and before long we have something like the kind of DHS document making all kinds of accusations with very little, if any, evidence to support their claims.

Please do not confuse what most people believe as governments' most important role of protecting its citizens (much like what the Bush administration did in the years after 9/11/2001) with government efforts to discourage expression of First Amendment rights by publishing a report that is replete with accusations, paranoia, and scare tactics, but lacking factual content. It seems that whenever liberals and the mainstream media want to cover an event or a protest that supports their agenda, they're all over it. For instance, as I mentioned previously, the media had no trouble covering the immigration demonstrations that took place all across the country a few years ago; every major media outlet in the country made sure it was a regular and significant part of their reporting. Since we all know that there is no one in government capable of being "radical extremists," we need not worry about the propaganda that they produce regarding illegal immigration, right?

How about this statement: "DHS … assesses that rightwing extremist group's frustration over a perceived lack of government action on illegal immigration has the potential to incite individuals or small groups toward violence."[96] What a great assessment, unfortunately for DHS, there is not just a "perceived lack of government action on illegal immigration" throughout the country, the threat from illegal immigration is actually real; yet we still get nothing but a bunch of government ineptitude. It is politically correct and acceptable to racially profile "rightwing extremists" since only "white" conservative people can be extremists. But when any other group of people is profiled there is hell to pay.

The DHS report includes this disturbing footnote in conclusion that states: "...that white supremacist lone wolves pose the most significant domestic terrorist threat because of their low profile and autonomy—separate from any formalized group—which hampers warning efforts."[97] There you have it, perfectly legitimate apparently to racially profile certain "radical extremists" without anyone taking notice; but we must not look at any other ethnic group as targets of "radical extremists" even though a large number of extremists in the world are anything but "white." I wonder how the Obama Administration would have characterized D.C. sniper John Allen Muhammad?

Near the end of the DHS report it states that "DHS...will be working with its state and local partners over the next several months to ascertain with greater regional specificity the rise in the rightwing extremist activity in the United States, with particular emphasis on the political, economic, and social factors that drive rightwing extremist radicalization."[98] There seems to be no doubt that the Department is referring to any and all types of "perceived" demonstrations by "radical extremists" such as those involved in the Tea Parties held across America. Make no mistake about it; the spread of government sanctioned propaganda contained in this horrible report would have us believe that they are only concerned with those demonstrations or positions that pose a threat to government from violent demonstrations of so called "radicals." Well, not to totally lose its sense of humor, the DHS report made this footnoted comment at the end of the report: "DHS encourages recipients of this document to report information concerning suspicious or criminal activity to DHS and the FBI."[99] Yeah, I'll get right on that.

I would have preferred that DHS not produced a document with the full blessing of the Obama administration; especially one that is so elementary in writing. Sadly, we are reduced to admitting that the document was not only sanctioned by Obama, but that it seems to be reflective of his ideals and philosophy.

I believe there are still plenty of conservatives, not the least of which include veterans who have served this country with honor, still waiting for President Obama to condemn the report, hand a pink slip to Napolitano, and insist that such a disgraceful report never find its way out of his administration again. And, oh yeah, an invitation to a beer summit at the White House where each veteran will receive the beverage of his choice, along with sincere apologies and gratitude from the Commander in Chief. No, I'm not kidding!

SUCCESS OR FAILURE

In early 2009, during the honeymoon period for President Obama, much was made in the media regarding whether Obama would succeed as president. The reason for the story surfacing the way it did and how the media had such a field day with it for so long can be attributed to Rush Limbaugh. During one of his radio broadcasts, Rush made it abundantly clear that he did not want Obama's liberal policies to see the light of day, or in other words, not succeed, which was (is) a reasonable position. You may recall that the basis for Rush's position was primarily, at least in part, due to a huge spending bill referred to as an economic stimulus package, supported almost exclusively by the democrats in Congress. Naturally, the initial remarks by Rush, and subsequent explanations to correct what the mainstream media had distorted, provided plenty of ammunition for many in the media to be overly critical of him. Anyone with a sliver of intelligence knows that Rush was expressing "hope and change" for Obama's liberal positions to fail because he believed they would be bad for the country; in that sense he did not want Obama to succeed. I would now like to spend some time exploring the concept of political success or failure in our society today, using the huge media circus surrounding Limbaugh's comment as impetus.

It never ceases to amaze me that many in the media and politicians like Mr. Obama deliberately spend time and effort to single out an extremely influential private citizen like Rush for the soul purpose of manipulating non-thinkers into believing that Rush or anyone who listens to him is evil if they want

Obama's policies to fail. This tactic from the left is typical of what often happens because they probably realize that they cannot win the battle of ideas. Naturally, the attack on Rush was taking place at a time when we were supposedly in the midst of the "worst economic crises since The Great Depression." That view is debatable, but with so many other pressing issues that seem to be heaped upon the shoulders of the president, it is absurd for him or anyone in his administration to give credence to comments by Rush Limbaugh. Although, it does seem to be proof that even Obama realizes the powerful influence Rush has in the political arena. Come to think of it, the president should probably be vigilant in his focus on Rush, because anything that takes him away from the damage he could be doing to the country by having some of his policies implemented is ultimately better for everyone else.

The double standard in the media has been talked about often by a host of fair-minded people, and many recognize that there is a different set of standards for reporting depending on which political ideology you happen to support. By the way, it is no magical secret that similar comments made by liberals concerning hopes that George W. Bush would fail were a non-factor as reported by the mainstream press. That is not surprising, only troubling because of the lack of service they are providing their viewers, listeners and readers. For instance: "On the morning of September 11, 2001, just minutes before learning of the terrorists attacks on America, Democrat strategist James Carville was hoping that President Bush failed, telling a group of Washington reporters: 'I certainly hope he doesn't succeed.' Carville was joined by democratic pollster Stanley Greenberg, who seemed encouraged by a survey he had just completed that revealed public misgivings about the newly minted president. 'We rush into these focus groups with these doubts that people have about him, and I'm wanting them to turn against him,' Greenberg admitted. Minutes later, as news of the terrorists attacks reached the hotel conference room where the democrats were having breakfast with the reporters, Carville announced: 'Disregard everything we just said! This changes everything!'"[100] Naturally, the press obliged! The difference between the comments by these two democrat strategist's and that of Rush Limbaugh can be evaluated by the casual observer, however, it is safe to say that Limbaugh's comment about Obama's policies failing received greater scrutiny and denouncement by the press than did Greenburg's or Carville's.

Is there any doubt that the lapdog press fell into lockstep with Carville? The comments by two stalwart liberals like Greenburg and Carville are demonstrative of the fact that such people seem to have a warped way of thinking; they say whatever is expedient with little to no fear of repercussion. Subsequently, the mainstream press had an opportunity to display the same "high" standards of journalism that were on display during the aftermath of the comments by Rush about President Obama; but sadly, Rush was not given equal treatment by the same media that looked the other way in light of the comments made by Carville and Greenberg about hoping Bush would not succeed. Anyone who knows the difference between day and night is not surprised when members of the media see only what they choose to see. I guess that's the new and improved "objectivity."

Perhaps it is also safe to say, but rarely if ever admitted to, that the mainstream media should not be surprised whenever they are accused of biased reporting. I think they have actually accepted the facts of their liberal leaning and would like to move on, if not for Fox News and conservative talk radio. Perhaps this little exercise will help: If you belong to the elite liberal leaning media, please repeat the following words after supplying appropriate acronyms such as CNN, ABC, CBS, NBC, MSNBC, etc. "I am a liberal and I work at (plug in the name of your network, even if you're convinced that what you do is objective reporting), a liberal media organization and defender of liberal politicians and policies, whether they actually make sense and benefit people or not." There, that feels better, huh?

Half of the battle of media bias substance abuse is admitting that there is a problem in the first place, which I suppose is why the liberal media is the way it is. By the way, if anyone is keeping score, any sort of conservative reporting that may take place in the media finally has some footing compared to the dominance of liberal reporting that has taken place for decades, especially when there was little or no competition for so many years. And let's not forget that there is a difference between the "news" compared to what is discussed on the many opinion shows, which nearly all network and cable stations air.

In addition to the pork-laden stimulus package passed by the Congress in 2009, and signed by the president, there were other issues that served as a core concern for many conservatives, and which were touted as being critical to the success or failure of the country, including, but not limited to: health care reform; the president announcing that he would close Guantanamo Bay in a year; nationalizing the banking system; problems at General Motors and Chrysler that involved firing a CEO; cap and trade; and the list could go on because that is just a sampling of what was happening in Obama's first few months in office! These concerns, and many others which will no doubt surface after the publication of this book, should pique the interests of all people, especially conservatives in general as well as members of Congress. The apparent frustration for many conservatives outside Washington is that many of us do not believe that there are enough elected officials on the national stage that have the guts to stand up for the kind of conservative values that will help all people, not just particular classes of people in our society. If you are an elected member of Congress and are too afraid to stand up and be a conservative leader, do us all a favor and leave office as soon as possible to make way for real conservatives who are not afraid to lead. Furthermore, the president must be willing to work with those who may not agree with all that he is trying to do. Dissent and disagreement are part of the process, but that must not halt the process of debate and compromise in government. And if conservatives are not invited to be a part of the process by the president or are ignored for the sake of an all day photo op, as in the case of the health care summit, then representative government is in jeopardy.

I believe that the lack of commitment to live and teach the conservative values embodied by Ronald Reagan is missing from the national stage in general. Nearly since Reagan left office, but certainly post-1994 and the "Contract with America," it seems that conservatives have often been content to blend in with everyone else. It is a mystery to me that the Republican Party, the standard bearer for conservative values, has had no real direction on a consistent basis to educate people about conservatism and its benefits for our society. Conservatives of late seem only too willing to govern like their liberal peers, and that is simply not good enough. There must be consistent and sustained effort by conservatives, as we cannot afford to allow liberalism to run amuck and just sit back and watch it happen.

Those who do not agree with such a statement need not take offense, it's nothing personal. Unfortunately, we may never have another Reagan in my lifetime. If that is the case, we need more people courageous enough to stand for principled conservatism, and who are willing to have the fortitude to stand up and be counted as Reagan did. I am committed to doing what is necessary and standing up for conservative principles that will foster the kind of attitude and reality that are needed to keep this country great. Conservatives cannot rely upon the media or anyone else to accurately convey to the people the ideals of conservatism when it comes to the success or failure of this country.

Those in the media like Chris Matthews, Keith Olbermann, Matt Lauer, and a host of others have the right to dispense the kind of information they see fit; just as Rush Limbaugh, Sean Hannity, and Glen Beck have the same right. Everyone knows that all these people subscribe to a particular political perspective and each group hopes for the other groups' failure relative to political philosophy. Disagreements will always abound but it does not mean that those disagreements equate to hate—failure of philosophy perhaps, but not hate.

Here is a pathetic example of what we do not need: "The Democratic National Committee has joined the administration's campaign against talk-host Rush Limbaugh, proposing to place an anti-Limbaugh billboard message in 'Rush Limbaugh's hometown of West Palm Beach, Florida.' The DNC placed a banner on its homepage inviting visitors to participate in a contest to determine what message of ten words or less will be placed on the billboard. After visitors complete a form and submit their entry, they are also invited to make a contribution to the DNC. The Web site declares: 'We'll go through all of the slogans you submit, and the winner will have his or her submission appear on a billboard in Rush Limbaugh's hometown of West Palm Beach, Florida—and receive a free T-shirt featuring the winning slogan.'"[101]

Oh, wow! A free t-shirt! What kind of pathetic, low budget prize is that? In any case, I am astounded that the committee for the Democratic Party could be so intoxicated over worrying about Rush, especially in light of the worst economic challenges our nation was facing "since The Great Depression." Is that not evidence that the DNC really does not care about moving an agenda forward that they say is supposed to help the very people they always claim to be fighting for? We can only imagine what would have happened to the Republican National Committee had they sponsored a similar contest featuring a prominent liberal. Please remember that the DNC joined efforts with the "administration's campaign against talk-host Rush Limbaugh." How embarrassing that the president cannot seem to take the criticism from a guy on the radio.

I have played a little basketball throughout my life, and I understand that the president enjoys a good game of hoops as well. Now this is probably reckless conjecture on my part, but if the president plays hoops like he governs, then I'm betting that he is the kind of player who calls every little ticky-tacky foul, but does not allow an opposing player to do the same thing, especially if he is involved in the play.

It is painfully obvious that liberals in government are not terribly concerned about moving the country forward like they so often preach to the rest of us. Behind the lip service, it just seems like they are trying to increase their position of absolute dominance of everything and everyone. Typically, conservatives espouse those things that will benefit the majority of society, that give individuals opportunities to succeed. The philosophy of most democrats is nothing new because it comes from a worn-out playbook called liberalism. The same old plays are tried again and again to demonize those who disagree with their pretended philosophy of feigning concern for the downtrodden, and all who have lost hope because they have been told there is none by liberals. Liberals may talk about self-reliance and working hard to get ahead in life; and make no mistake, they know what they are doing and it is actually counter to any sort of productivity advocated by conservatism. Liberals had a bump in the road in 1994, but that was nothing more than a temporary setback.

The interesting reality concerning liberalism is that it has pretended to be the economic prosperity champion of the poor and middle class for far too long. And what do we have to show for it? We have many in society largely dependent upon the government for retirement, health care for seniors that is on the verge of being bankrupted, a newly passed piece of health care legislation that will likely follow the same course, an entitlement philosophy that has dominated the taxpayer-sponsored federal budget for decades, big unions that have over-stepped their usefulness and must share in the blame for the weak automotive industry in the US, and in general, an apathetic attitude in government and among the governed that has reached an unhealthy proportion.

The sad truth is that liberal policies only seem to help those succeed to whom they matter most: the liberal politicians who advocate them in the first place! If government-sponsored welfare, healthcare, or retirement were so wonderful and good, would we be in any of the pitiful predicaments we now face concerning either one of them? The answer is obvious because it is difficult to name one beneficial liberal social program that has actually worked in the last hundred years. Liberals and conservatives alike have permitted the near bankrupt nature of entitlements by continuous manipulation of the electorate on one side and failure to advocate meaningful reform on the other. I must emphasize that I'm in favor of making sure that the vulnerable in our society are taken care of. Obviously though, there are a lot of people who I would not identify as vulnerable in our society who have bought into the entitlement philosophy and now believe that the government owes them.

Beginning with every fiscally irresponsible president from FDR to now; as well as every fiscally irresponsible Congress from that time until now, we have been saddled with dysfunctional spending policies that very few politicians have had the guts to tackle because of that annoyance they refer to as the next election. And it must be noted that over the same span, democrats have been in control of the Congress for the majority of those years. Bottom line: the status quo has become the acceptable way among many democrats and republicans in Washington, no matter how often they talk about cracking down on fraud, waste, and abuse. They have had more than enough time to have changed the status quo if that is what they really wanted to do.

Once upon a time there was an incessant cry out of Washington lamenting the fact that Social Security was going to be bankrupted if something was not done to remedy the situation. I seem to remember that as far back as the Clinton years, there were many who advocated that the Congress fix Social Security in order to avert crises. It seems that only George W. Bush had the guts to propose reforming Social Security in order to keep it solvent, in a way that would not affect those already receiving payments, and also those for whom payments would begin relatively soon. Bush even talked of privatizing part of Social Security for younger workers to give them greater control and options for growth. Even though he may not have had the best idea about how to reform Social Security, Bush at least was willing to try, because that's what a leader does.

Naturally, a democrat-controlled Congress scoffed at the notion of reforming Social Security. In typical fashion, liberals proposed no real changes to Social Security that would keep it solvent for decades to come. That sounds eerily like maintaining the status quo. Is solvency really the ultimate goal of Social Security? The democrats used the "fear card" to work many seniors into a hissy about potentially not receiving their monthly payments because Bush was going to take it away from them.

Whether the issue of Social Security reform is resurrected under a Congress that is democrat controlled remains to be seen. Although, if liberals continue to adhere to their track record, questions of solvency in Social Security and other unfunded entitlements will continue to exist, nothing more than subsidized failure by you and me. I could care less where credit is given for any kind of governmental reform regarding entitlements; just get it done for the sake of the taxpayers who have to fund them!

I want to make sure that I am not being misunderstood about what I think should be done with Social Security. My parents were born in the late 1930s. Obviously, I did not experience the Great Depression and World War II, and my parent's experiences were limited to that of childhood during an actual time of real crisis. But their parents certainly experienced the full effects of both the Depression and WWII as adults. Arguably, the decades of the 1930s and 1940s were two of the most challenging that the United States has ever had to endure. I'm glad I did not have to experience that part of American history firsthand.

One of the biggest challenges regarding Social Security is going to be overcoming the attitude that Social Security is now generally accepted as a right in America; it has simply been allowed to be too much of a predominant aspect of our national budget, instead of something designed to be temporary. I cannot imagine that anyone believes that the Social Security retirement system was ever destined to be a long-term form of retirement for America's seniors. Moreover, because of the heinous nature of entitlements, everyone knows that solving the problems associated with Social Security reform will also require the determination and fortitude of a Congress and president with the backbone and courage to make the changes that are necessary and ultimately better. "We the people" want to see our elected representatives begin doing the right thing when it comes to Social Security reform; as well as other entitlement reforms that are overdue. And to be certain, I am not advocating taking the retirement network provided by Social Security away from those most at jeopardy in our society.

Naturally, there is a need for a security net for the disabled and those vulnerable in our society who cannot provide for themselves without assistance. We would be a cold and heartless nation to turn our backs on those not able to provide for themselves; but that does not mean that you roll the red carpet out for everyone else who is capable. So our attention must be focused on the millions of people that reach retirement age and have been able to work and set aside funds to provide for their own quality of life after retirement; those who will not need government assistance to live out the remainder of their golden years. I do not believe the government should be assisting older workers who can pay for the bulk of their health care, prescription drugs and other retirement necessities on their own. However, it is obvious that many seniors have paid into Social

Security for a number of years so what do we do for the people who have paid into the program with the greatest amount of funds? That is a challenging question to answer and no matter how it is resolved it will probably make more than a few people upset. The approach with younger workers may not be as difficult since they have less at stake. For everyone else a gradual change in the attitude about Social Security must focus on the shift from the idea that Social Security is regarded as a right.

Regardless of the approach, many people may feel betrayed by a government that withholds funds from their paycheck to pay for those capable of taking care of themselves. The primary focus should be on helping the vulnerable and making sure that the system will actually be solvent for those future generations. I wonder what people did before anyone entertained the idea of a social safety net for the people of America. I guess they just prepared for their own retirement needs all by themselves, what a concept. Personally, I have no expectations of getting anything from Social Security when the time comes. There is a way to lighten the burden of those paying the tax, yet still provide for those in need of retirement assistance. I'm willing to forfeit my Social Security benefits to those who are most in need of it.

I support paying a level or even reduced portion in Social Security taxes upon an independent audit of the system to determine who actually needs the monthly payment, such as continuing to provide some piece of mind for those in our society who are unable to make it on their own because of disability, disease, or some other equally devastating circumstance. Whatever pain the process of fixing Social Security may produce, ultimately, if reducing the tax liability of America's workers is achieved, while still taking care of those in need; then over the long term, it will have been worth it.

Getting people weaned off Social Security who do not need it must be the ultimate goal. It will require people (especially those past retirement age) to adopt a new mindset, primarily, that the government should never have been involved in the retirement security of its citizens to begin with. Those who have good health and are capable of working and providing for their own retirement may have the most difficult time accepting the fact that they will not receive a government check for a few hundred dollars each month or government payment for prescription drugs upon retirement.

Younger workers should be content knowing that they will be able to keep more of their money, because of meaningful reform, to invest and save for their retirement since the government will be taking less money from them over the course of the rest of their working years. Obviously, new workers entering the workforce stand the most to gain by having a reduced Social Security tax liability, and must then take a more active role in their personal retirement nest egg. Ultimately, all citizens stand to gain from reforming Social Security. Those who are in need will continue to receive the benefit, however, those who have been able to provide for their own retirement will also benefit by having taken the steps to ensure their own wellbeing. And for young workers just starting out, they will have ample time to plan, invest, and save for a retirement that may be as far as forty or more years away. In order for any plan to be successful, the key components are government control of spending and actually cutting spending in unproductive taxpayer-funded failures, not to mention the personal responsibility of citizens to save, invest, control spending and curtail debt as much as possible.

Social Security reform is an issue that could potentially redefine the way our government functions with respect to its fiduciary responsibility over the people's money. The billions upon billions of dollars wasted by our government must stop if we are to see any meaningful spending reform, not only with Social Security, but all entitlement programs that the government gluts itself on. It is more than just reforming policies and programs that will determine our success or failure because there must be a complete reformation of the pervasive attitudes that have created the worst kind of dependency our nation has probably ever seen, especially now as we have witnessed even businesses with palms turned up for a bailout.

Reforming Social Security will be difficult when democrats control the Legislative and Executive branches of government. And it does not bode well for reform knowing that successful continuation of poorly managed entitlements of any kind are inextricably intertwined with the Democratic Party. But reform can be achieved with the right attitude and approach. Like anyone who has had children knows, in order for our children to stand on their own, we must sever the ties of dependency and encourage them to make it without us because we are ultimately doing them a favor by teaching them to be independent. If "we the people" are going to succeed, government must do what is necessary to reform Social Security and all entitlements.

Medicare has even engendered dependency by those who have been successful in their own right by making it too easy for seniors to be enrolled in the program even if there is not a financial need; but anyone who suggests that these seniors take care of their personal medical healthcare costs on their own is portrayed as uncaring and mean-spirited. You might be thinking the same thing: why should frail but capable old folks have to worry about medical costs in the golden years of life? Well, all I can say is that it's not hard to understand how we have become a dependent society; we act as if we are owed something just because we have reached a certain age. I hate to burst any bubbles, but none of us is owed anything by virtue of the fact that we occupy space on this planet. All we should expect is to be free to pursue life, liberty, and happiness. And government needs to figure out how to stay out of it so everyone can pursue what the founding fathers intended, uninhibited.

Mr. Obama has "promised a more intensive effort to weed inefficient and bloated programs out of the federal budget in the short run, creating a White House position to scour this budget, line by line, eliminating what we don't need, or what *doesn't* work, and improving the things that do."[102] I am in agreement with the president. Eliminating wasteful government spending will benefit the country as a whole, and in the process strengthen Mr. Obama's chances for a second term in office. However, most of us are beyond the talking stage when it comes to anyone in government actually doing something to eliminate wasteful spending. And with President Obama, he says whatever he wants to say even if it is in direct contradiction to what he said as Senator Obama during the campaign of 2008. We have yet to see meaningful elimination of that which "we don't need" as promised by the president, and in fact have seen efforts to expand even further those things "we don't need" by the Congress and president.

Why is it so difficult for politicians in Washington to understand the positive outcome of reducing taxes and eliminating wasteful entitlement spending or earmarks as they have come to be called? All politicians, including the president, seem to be tiptoeing around the issue of any meaningful reform even though, in particular, the president seems to enjoy talking about what needs to be done. Unfortunately, talking about reform or what needs to be done does not mean it is going to actually happen; or more especially, happen in the right way. But talking seems to be what many politicians do best.

I challenge anyone elected to represent the people to pick an entitlement program to reform or eliminate altogether. It only takes one person to pick one program, introduce legislation to begin the process, and then let the debates begin. If performed with the interests of the people above their own self-interests; real reform or elimination of wasteful spending associated with entitlements will be the end product. Just think of the legacy that could be passed on to future generations of representatives; not to mention the kind of precedent for getting things done in Washington, D.C. A huge hurdle to reform seems to be that politicians spend too much time concerning themselves over which party gets credit for the good that might be accomplished, if any good is ever accomplished. It seems that

practically no one has a problem pointing the finger of blame
toward those for whom things are perceived as wrong. Many in
Washington seem to be a lot like the pigs in *Animal Farm!*
You may remember that in the beginning of the animal
rebellion in the book *Animal Farm,* the pigs asserted themselves
as the de facto rulers of the farm. Through a series of events
over time, the other animals were obliged to defer to the pigs in
every instance involving leadership questions. The pigs quickly
began to dominate, and once they made it to the big farm house
and recognized all the perks associated with that experience
(even though they loathed such things before because of their
contempt for humans), they considered themselves to be above
their animal peers. The pigs asserted control over the other animals and insisted that they get credit for the good that came
to all the animals on the farm, and in fact, through a series of
manipulative and secretive modifying of the rules, they were
able to strengthen that control. Yes, it is evident that like the
pigs in *Animal Farm,* politicians today care more about where
credit is placed in Washington than whether or not the policies
enacted are beneficial and actually best serve to promote the
success of all citizens.

For too many years in American politics, we have witnessed
the "us against them" mentality that seems to also be pervasive
among many of the people as well. It is difficult to determine
exactly when this attitude began to take on a life of its own.
Perhaps it goes back to the days of our founding. It might even
go back even farther than that. I suppose that from the beginning of time there has always been an "opposition party," and
I suppose there probably always will be. But I want to know
when government decided to take upon itself the notion that
it had to be the "pigs" on the farm, so to speak. Obviously, the
evolution of modern-day liberalism has its underpinnings in the
1930s, which was the foundation for what I like to refer to as
the time that ushered in the age of "dependency." There is no
justification for continuing to increase the level of entitlements

in the twenty-first century. A government that continues to do things for those who are fully capable of taking care of their own needs does not make sense to those of us who believe in personal responsibility.

As a conservative, I believe that the way to achieve and maintain economic prosperity and success centers on those things that stimulate economic growth in the first place, namely job creation, wealth creation, favorable tax rates to include reduced capital gains taxes, sensible regulation, and ethics at all levels of business and government. Less government involvement in our capitalistic system is usually always good in determining the long term and consistent success of our economy amidst the ever present ups and downs we will often experience. During the Great Depression, had there been a more concerted effort to quickly reduce taxes, for instance, making it easier for businesses and individuals to meet necessary obligations, the duration and severity of the Depression may have been dramatically reduced.

I believe the reason why so many people disagreed with the democrat-controlled Congress and Mr. Obama, with respect to the level of government involvement during the economic crises he "inherited," was due to the fact that many people simply could not justify the level of spending without regard to any sense of control. As of this writing, it remains to be seen what sort of economic impact throwing billions of dollars of good money after bad will have on the economy. It is clear that the "stimulus" plan did not create or save the amount of jobs that Obama preached that it would. In fact, many millions of people have lost their jobs since Obama became president. And because of the near impossibility to account for all that money, it is easy for Obama and anyone else who supports such a plan to attribute any rebound in the economy to the "stimulus plan." And it was not many months after the passing of the largest spending bill in history for Obama to say that it was working. You see, he can say what he wants and it will not matter to those who have an infatuation for the man. I believe that Mr. Obama will probably always be given the benefit of the doubt, which is more than I can say about any republican president in recent memory.

Anyone remotely familiar with the ebb and flow of our economy knows that the nature of our economic system does not require a genius to figure out that what goes down will eventually come up. Saying that the economic stimulus package is doing its job only serves to perpetuate the support of ignorance that Obama already enjoys. Reckless spending by bureaucrats must be controlled because our government's treasury cannot continue to print money and have people think that things will be fine. I want to know where all the whiners are who incessantly complained about deficit spending under republican administrations but who have not uttered a peep with the kind of record-setting deficit spending we have witnessed to this point. I believe that during an economic decline, the last thing you should be doing is printing more money because of the devaluating factor. Instead of printing more and more money, the government ought to be concentrating on being good stewards of the current money supply by cutting taxes and controlling spending. "We the people" must insist upon it.

Another school of thought regarding what will promote success or failure in our government is centered around the impact of too much government interference on the economy. I want to re-emphasize some of the things that tend to destabilize our economy and lead to certain failure: One: unreasonably high tax rates which lead to a lack of incentive to be productive. Two: government efforts to redistribute wealth that leads to less wealth creation. Three: too much governmental regulation and involvement. Four: unethical behavior at all levels of business and government.

I have to believe that most Americans who work for a living recognize the principles that engender economic prosperity within their own families and that they know the way to get ahead is to live within their means. Saving and investing money for retirement, having some cash on hand for emergencies, being ethical while earning a living, and transacting legitimate business with others are just a few easy ways to get and stay ahead. I do not think it is too much to ask that our government do the same thing that every individual and family in America is expected to do. The IRS is certainly one of those government entities that demands full compliance and accountability to the tax code; so we should expect no less from government since it has a responsibility to spend the money it receives from "we the people" in the most efficient manner possible.

Most people encounter economic hardship at one point or another in their lives, and even though there may be situations beyond our control such as illness, loss of employment, or natural disaster; oftentimes, the economic challenges we experience are brought about by the tendency to overspend. If we choose to pay for the things we "want" today by leveraging the income we expect to receive in the future, we open ourselves up to challenges. We all want to be regarded as reasonably intelligent when it comes to money matters, but too often we lose the ability to think rationally when money is involved. It has happened to me as well, but admitting that we have problems budgeting money can help us overcome being uptight and embarrassed that we have put ourselves in a bind in the first place. Most people would be embarrassed and ashamed to admit that they are upside down in their personal finances. But that does not seem to bother the government, it does not seem to care about the spending imbalance it has incurred.

The only way out of such a situation for individuals is to bite the bullet and rectify the imbalance of our economic setback by cutting back and making the necessary spending sacrifices until we get ourselves back into a position where assets outweigh liabilities. It probably seems like an extremely outrageous notion to expect our government to be good stewards of the people's money and to cut spending where it needs to be cut, but if we all managed our personal finances as irresponsibly as the government, we would all be up the often traveled creek with no paddle unless we make changes that are essential for our continued economic prosperity.

From the time I was born to the present the government's solution to practically every problem, be it social, economic, or otherwise is to just keep allocating huge sums of money in the hope that things will improve, and no amount of regulation or legislation has seemed to be effective. Well, the question that we and our elected representatives have to ask is: How well has that approach worked? Many liberals would have us believe that the more money government sets aside for a host of issues, the better. I want to point out a couple of areas where more is not necessarily better. First, how many billions upon billions of dollars have been spent over the last fifty years, indeed, that continue to be spent on failing public schools in America? Has the government been able to remotely justify, let alone qualify, the success of its schools? How much of the "dumbing down" of the curriculum just to move students through the system are we going to continue to accept? With so many unanswered questions, here is perhaps the most distressing one. Why is the government still involved in the business of educating our young people? And why do we keep electing people who we know will continue to advocate the subsidizing of failure just for the sake of retaining power over the people?

I propose this analogy. When I was in elementary school, we lived on a dairy farm in Indiana. Even though my siblings and I were young, we were still expected to do as much work as our little bodies could handle, and as far as I was concerned, that seemed like quite a bit, though I must say that it has not affected me in an adverse way because it taught me the value of work at an early age, even though I may not have always appreciated it. One of the things that I observed about dairy cattle, even at a tender age was that they live up to their "herd mentality" label because most often if one cow tried to squeeze into a particular opening or area, the cows near by would try to do the same thing. For instance, when milking time came around my brothers and I were often responsible for herding the cows into the holding area; normally easy enough since cows at least instinctively seem to know when milking time rolls around. If you have never been around dairy cattle, you may be inclined to believe that getting them into the holding area could be described as the most blissful part of the experience, and you would be absolutely correct in my opinion.

The system of milking that we employed allowed for four cows to be milked at one time, each confined to an individual stall. In order to get the cows from the holding pen to the milking position, each cow had to take her turn filing up a ramp from outside and then wait for the door to open so that she could proceed to the next available stall in the milk house. Well, the sooner a cow could move into a stall, the sooner she could be milked and begin enjoying a ration of grain. When the door to the milk house opened to allow a cow to enter, occasionally more than one cow would try and squeeze through the doorway.

Usually they somehow corrected it themselves, but on those occasions, when they did not, my father would often shout out a few choice expletives that seemed to put the fear of the devil into the cows involved and one would quickly make her way into the milk house while the others maintained a measure of contentment while waiting for the next available opening. And you could only pray that a disturbed cow that had been previously yelled at would not end up kicking my father while being prepped for milking, because a beating would surely ensue. Of course, no one knew any better back then about the psychological damage done to a cow for being contrary. After every cow was milked, the same scenario presented itself a mere twelve hours later when the cows had to be milked again.

It seems that with most things handled by the government, "herd mentality" is often the model for doing business. Politicians continue to allocate funds to those things that are clearly not working for the benefit of "we the people." Just like the "herd mentality" with cows, government often does not know when to hold back either, at least with cows you can expect chaos because they're animals for crying out loud! But politicians are a different breed altogether, and they often do not seem to have sense enough to pull back and scrap policies and programs that are just not working. I remember seeing my father beat the living hell out of a cow (if that's possible) for not cooperating at milking time. I am not necessarily advocating the same type of treatment for politicians, but the electorate has to ensure that useless politicians are beaten at the ballot box and then continue to hold those elected to be responsible. We cannot continue to turn a blind eye to what elected politicians are doing to our country. Too often we only get the lip service from politicians with regard to issues like education, tax reform, and some of the fiscally irresponsible entitlement programs I have already mentioned; all of which if left unchecked will lead to inevitable failure.

In the previous chapter, I made reference to this quote from President Obama: "We need to level the playing field for workers and the unions that represent their interests ... I do not view the labor movement as part of the problem. To me, it's part of the solution ... You cannot have a strong middle class without a strong labor movement."[103] The reason I mention this quote again is to illustrate how liberals seem to enjoy pitting one class of people against another because class envy seems to be a very integral part of the Democratic Party. A few months after making his comments about leveling "the playing field," Mr. Obama said "that he's working toward a simpler tax code that rewards work and the pursuit of the American dream. For too long, we've seen taxes used as a wedge to scare people into supporting policies that increased the burden on working people instead of helping them live their dreams ... We need to simplify a monstrous tax code that is far too complicated for most Americans to understand, but just complicated enough for the insiders who know how to game the system."[104]

With such statements about taxes the president seemed *gung ho* for simplifying the tax code. I think that would be great and would be something most of us could all support. His approach is to simplify the tax code so it "rewards work and the pursuit of the American dream," but how has he suggested ways in which this simplification will take place? We are fast approaching the point in this country where nearly 50% of workers pay little to no income taxes at all. As a matter of fact, we know, according to IRS statistics for 2006: "Some 45.6 million tax filers—one-third of all filers—have no federal income tax liability after taking credits and deductions."[105]

It seems to me that there is no reason for Obama to push for reforming the tax code since he wants a tax code that "rewards work." Near as I can tell, it appears that our current tax code is quite friendly and "rewards work" already for over forty-five million tax filers. Could it be that the very people Obama talks about helping are already being taken care of by the current tax system and that it makes no sense for him to be pontificating about reforming a tax code that is already benefiting them! It is time for more of the American people to wake up and take the Tea Parties to the next level by getting rid of status quo politicians.

It is clear that Obama has a narrow view on who he actually thinks should be sharing in the "American dream." I believe that the tax code in its current form is not only unfair to the people who provide the jobs for the rest of us, but to everyone else above a certain income level trying to make a living as well. Mr. Obama has said that, "It will take time to undo the damage of years of carve-outs and loopholes. But I want every American to know that we will rewrite the tax code so that it puts your interests over any special interest. And we will make it quicker, easier, and less expensive for you to file a return ..."[106] Ambitious plan, and one in which we have been waiting for years and years to have actually happen. I wonder if Obama realizes that by eliminating the "carve-outs and loopholes" he will actually alienate himself from some of the members of his own party, particularly members of his Cabinet. Other than that, I would like to know who the "your" is when Obama says he is going to put "your interests over any special interest." Perhaps he considers the people who provide the jobs to the rest of us as "special interests." We already know that many liberals harbor contempt for big oil, pharmaceuticals, Wall Street, and the CEO's who run the companies of many industries.

As a nation, we are sacrificing our future success because of the malicious nature of some of our politicians. The way for everyone to achieve success in our country is by all able-bodied people securing gainful employment that provides for the needs, and ultimately, some of the wants of their families. Government can best help in this effort by allowing hard working Americans to keep as much of what they earn, thus creating a greater incentive to work in the first place. I think most people would agree that politicians have enjoyed too much success talking out of both sides of their mouths for far too long.

I do not believe that our founding fathers ever anticipated that politicians were to be elected so that they could get whatever they want over what is best for the people. It seems to me that we are clearly at a moment in American politics that "we the people" must stand united against a corrupt body of leaders that seem to be doing their best to bring down the greatness of America. The United States of America is a country that has done more for other nations than any other country on the face of the earth. We must be vigilant in our efforts to go on the offensive at election time and fight against those whose policies weaken our sovereignty as a nation.

WAIT, WHAT?

Every generation can be credited for establishing particular statements or sayings that could be characterized as nothing more than clichés that everyone usually picks up on. For instance, here are a few from the seventies: Groovy, Far Out, Right On, and Say What? Like most clichés, it is difficult to ascertain who should get the credit, or the blame, for coming up with such sayings in the first place; nevertheless, it does not take long for these generationally created phrases to be used by most people from coast to coast. And like most sayings in the English language, they often have a way of making a comeback and getting repeated by subsequent generations. Well, because I have a teenage daughter, I guess I need to give her credit for the idea behind the title of this chapter, because I believe it is appropriate; and hopefully, you will too.

One day, while talking to my daughter about possible titles for this book, she was not all that impressed with some of the titles that I was coming up with. She actually wanted the title of this chapter to be the title for the book. As a parent, I had to draw the line. Of course, there is a little more to the story. I had the opportunity of teaching an early morning religion class to a group of high school-aged young people prior to the start of their regular school day, using Scripture as the text for the class.

At one point in the middle of my last year of teaching the class, I noticed that a couple of the students seemed to be wearing out the phrase: *wait, what?* It always seemed to be used whenever one of the students failed to hear something that had been said in class or that they simply disbelieved. Since my daughter was in the class too, I took it upon myself to ask her, out of the class if she had noticed how often that phrase was used during the fifty minute class period. After some brief contemplation and discussion with me, she eventually agreed that "*Wait, what?*" did seem to be getting a little worn-out in our class. So I decided to turn the tables on the students by using the phrase myself as a way of helping them to realize how often it was getting used in class. We actually had some fun with it as some of the students had not really paid much attention to how often they used the phrase, or how often they heard it used by their peers, on television sitcoms, or wherever.

I often use humor in many situations throughout day-to-day living to maintain sanity and good mental health considering what we are sometimes subjected to. The bottom line is that we need to laugh more, especially at ourselves. Unfortunately, it is sometimes difficult with politicians to find any humor regarding the things that they do, not to mention that they are seldom prone to laughing at themselves. Personally, if I did not laugh about some of the unbelievable shenanigans that take place among our elected officials, I would go absolutely berserk. Yet, that does not mean I am any less committed about getting rid of unscrupulous politicians who ought to be remanded to private life. Think about all the times you have heard a politician say something on TV, radio, or that you read and then asked yourself: *Did he just say what I think he said?* As unbelievable as it may sound, the next time you hear a politician say something outrageous, two words should automatically come to your mind: *Wait, what?*

I have intentionally saved the following portion of this book to the end because it epitomizes the unrelenting nature of some politicians and members of the media who want to do some of the most outrageous things imaginable regardless of the voice of the people. Many of us are aware of the devious efforts by liberals to silence the opposition by taking control of the radio air waves, for instance. Here is only a small sampling of what I am talking about.

"I think it's absolutely time to pass a standard. Now, whether it's called the Fairness Standard or whether it's called something else—I absolutely think it's time to be bringing accountability to the airwaves. Our new president has talked rightly about accountability and transparency; that we all have to step up and be responsible. And I think in this case, there needs to be some accountability and standards put in place."[107] This quote comes to us courtesy an interview by Bill Press of Democratic Senator Debbie Stabenow. As a member of the media, Press could not help himself during the interview and offered such ideas like: "Conservatives should not be the only voices heard on talk radio."[108] See what I mean about how difficult it is to distinguish the mainstream media from some liberals. It's hard to distinguish the interviewer from the interviewee. Before I continue with more of this incoherent drabble, let's talk Marketing 101; primarily for the benefit of Ms. Stabenow and Mr. Press.

The tricky thing about marketing reality is that there is a built-in mechanism to market liberal talk radio to anyone wishing to tune in; it is known as the free market, which I realize often grates on some liberals because they often view as part of their philosophical mission to think for people so that they are not troubled with having to do so on their own. Let me just say that we already have "accountability and transparency" on the radio, but where we need it even more is among members of Congress and certain members of the media in their dealings with the people. I have tried to make that message the centerpiece throughout this book, and hopefully I have succeeded. Mr. Press continues by asking the Senator: "Can we count on you to push for some hearings in the Senate this year, to bring these owners in and hold them accountable?" To which the Senator replies: "I have already had some discussions with colleagues and, you know, I feel like that's going to happen."[109] Wait, what? It seems evident that this little exchange is a miserable microcosm of an insidious effort by liberals who are desirous to do whatever they have to do in order to isolate people who may disagree with them, and then make them conform or attempt to silence them forever.

It is no laughing matter that the people who are currently in charge of our government, starting with the president, have some of the most radical ideas that, if implemented, will have an incredibly adverse impact upon our society for a long time to come. Here is the proverbial icing on the cake gush from Press: "I'm not a big fan of bringing back the Fairness Doctrine. But if station owners won't act on their own to offer a mix of voices on the radio, this Congress and this new administration will find a way to force them to do so. And the sooner, the better."[110] No, of course Press is not interested in "bringing back the Fairness Doctrine." What could possibly give anyone the idea that Press is interested in silencing viewpoints that may be in stark contradiction to his own? I cannot imagine that he is in favor of eliminating certain ideas from finding an audience! In reality, his major concern seems to be in regard to how soon we can get these hearings under way on Capitol Hill so he can get his popcorn and sit in the front row to watch it all happen.

I would hate to see how he might act if he was really interested in bringing back the "Fairness Doctrine." Well, let me be of some assistance to Mr. Press. First, if conservative talk radio is not for you, there are lots of other talk shows and stations playing all sorts of different music genres so just find another station. Second, with some effort, find the liberal voices on the radio so that you can listen to the kind of political thought you enjoy without denying me the same privilege. Third, please do not be foolish by advocating going after the station owners whom you believe are restricting liberal voices, because then you will be forced to go after the "country" stations that do not play "rock;" the "classic rock" stations that do not play "hip hop;" or any number of other stations that "market" to a specific demographic.

Last I checked we still live in the American free market, which means that station owners are going to put on the radio those programs that will attract the most profitable marketing dollars for themselves, which in turn provides the most exposure for the businesses that pay for it. I'm sure the distinguished Senator from Michigan and the incomparable Bill Press must believe that it's time for all the radio stations in the land to come clean and be more diverse in what they allow to be played on their stations. After all, I thought it was about "Fairness."

Conservatives, to my knowledge, have never called for liberals to be more conservative or to demand that liberal venues require an equal share of time devoted to conservative principles. America means freedom, not indoctrination. Perhaps some liberals need a refresher course on what it means to be free. Perhaps they would rather live somewhere else in the world, a place where things are more controlled. Might I suggest a quaint little island about ninety miles off the coast of Florida? And if you happen to take a boat, don't be shocked at all the laughing and finger pointing coming from those heading north.

I would like to end where I began by recognizing the significance of the founding fathers in contrast to the times we now live. Can you imagine any of the founding fathers or our first president, George Washington, making a comment like this: "In America, there is a failure to appreciate Europe's leading role in the world. Instead of celebrating your dynamic union and seeking to partner with you to meet common challenges, there have been times where America has shown arrogance and been dismissive, even derisive."[III] Wait, what? I am curious about a time when Europe has ever assumed a "leading role in the world" in accomplishing good for others, particularly in the last one hundred years. On the contrary, I seem to recall that the United States has come to the aid of Europe on more than a few occasions, not to mention the stability we provided through the decades after World War II. The US took a leading role in providing the kind of security that was needed after the war, and having not done so, the European continent would likely not

227

only look a lot different geographically, but probably not have enjoyed the fruits of a free society all these years. I have nothing against Europe, since my ancestors eventually made their way from that continent to this country. But the president of the United States making a speech in Europe should have inspired Obama to talk about the greatness of America and where the rest of the world would be today if not for the goodness, sacrifice, and dedication of some very decent people. We do not need our president deriding the very nation that "we the people" gave him the honor to preside over as president. It seems apparent that forty-four is more concerned about trying to talk his way to success, while apparently making appeasement the hallmark of his presidency.

While in Europe, Mr. Obama also seemed to have forgotten these very appropriate words: "When in the course of human events, it becomes necessary for one people to dissolve the political bands which have connected them with another, and to assume among the powers of the earth, the separate and equal station to which the Laws of Nature and of Nature's God entitle them, a decent respect to the opinions of mankind requires that they should declare the causes which impel them to the separation."[112]

As a new nation, we made every effort to not only "dissolve the political bands" that connected us to Europe but the founding fathers recognized their moral obligation to "declare the causes which impel them to the separation;" meaning, that there was strong motivation for the pioneers of freedom and independence to separate themselves from tyranny and become a new sovereign nation. The president missed a great opportunity while among Europeans to emphasize the good that is uniquely American, and instead made the choice to apologize for America's "arrogance" because he believes that it is somehow our fault for the challenges the world is now facing. If you ask me, that sort of behavior is not only not presidential, but also not American.

I am hopeful that by the end of Mr. Obama's first term in office that he will have not put our nation in a position of weakness and vulnerability because of his tendency to emphasize all that is supposedly wrong with America. That is not leadership. Fortunately, every few years Americans have the opportunity to go to the polls to make choices adjusting the balance of power in government. "We the people" must not continue to allow our future and the future of our children to be jeopardized by those whose narrow ambition in life is to amass all the power that their finite minds can comprehend. We must be prepared to defend all that is good and right about the Constitution, because that is the foundation for all that is good and right about America.

To quote a portion of one of our most beloved patriotic hymns: "Land where my fathers died, Land of the pilgrims' pride, from every mountain side Let freedom ring! Let mortal tongues awake; let all that breathe partake. Protect us by thy might, Great God, our King!"[113] It is time for all those who love freedom and liberty to unite and defeat every attempt, foreign or domestic to destroy our Constitution before it has been wrestled from "we the people" by seemingly legitimate legal means. And accordingly, if you are breathing, you should be participating.

As a people, we must be aware of those who attempt to weaken or subvert the Constitution, to make it irrelevant based upon the notion of a sense of greater evolved ability to render it useless based upon subsequent laws. Laws created since the establishment of the Constitution, especially in the modern era, have usually never been an adequate barometer for making correct decisions or interpretations because in most instances laws that have been created are the consequence of the abandonment of time-tested moral behavior. Acceptable moral behavior should not flow from the judicial bench or by deference to laws made by the very people who have sworn an oath to "protect" and "defend" the Constitution. Every law we are bound by today does not necessarily have a moral foundation.

Since we are a nation governed by laws, we must understand that our nation's laws are only as strong as the moral fiber of the Legislator's who have established them, and the people who ultimately sustain them. In other words, the law must never be allowed to supersede the moral underpinnings of a God-fearing people. And we would do well to remember that it was a God-fearing people, inspired to establish the Constitution, who believed that there is such a thing as right and wrong, that laws should not be created or made to justify the immoral conduct of a civilized society.

EPILOGUE

To describe the current state of political affairs as fluid and ever-changing would perhaps be the understatement of the century. It is impossible to write a book about contemporary politics in the United States without experiencing, often extreme, changes, or at least proposed changes that if adopted would be extreme. As I have stated previously, it was also impossible for our founding fathers to anticipate the kind of corruption that now exists among many of our elected representatives. This is troubling because there can be no greater honor for a politician than to serve the people for whom trust has been granted. And if that trust has been violated, a price must be paid.

In the *Federalist Papers, Number 23*, Alexander Hamilton makes this observation relative to the potential for corruption of unchecked power by the federal government: "Every view we may take of the subject, as candid inquirers after truth, will serve to convince us, that it is both unwise and dangerous to deny the federal government an unconfined authority, as to all those objects which are entrusted to its management. It will indeed deserve the most vigilant and careful attention of the people, to see that it be modeled in such a manner as to admit of its being safely vested with the requisite powers. If any plan which has been, or may be, offered to our consideration, should not, upon a dispassionate inspection, be found to answer this description, it ought to be rejected. A government, the constitution of which renders it unfit to be trusted with all the powers which a free people ought to delegate to any government, would be an unsafe and improper depositary of the national interests."

The key to the best opportunity for the success of "we the people" under our system of government is to ensure that we take a proper accounting of those elected to make laws for the rest of us. They must remain unfettered by their personal emotion and bias. Quite often, politicians do not do things that are best for us. The health care debate in this country unleashed great interests among the people to the point of "the most vigilant and careful attention of the people." This sort of concern and expression by the people is exactly what is necessary in America regardless of how some politicians and media members often characterize such vigilance by the people. There must be civil dialogue among politicians and the people. Shouting down by either side is counter to progress.

Freedom in a republic such as ours carries with it the necessity for personal responsibility and accountability. Reckless and irresponsible behavior must not continue to be rewarded in our form of government. Politicians must ever be vigilant to remember from whom they received their power to act. And the people must be equally vigilant in demanding that all politicians remain accountable for that power.

ENDNOTES

BY THE PEOPLE, FOR THE PEOPLE

1 "The Declaration of Independence of the United States of America."

2 Ibid.

3 Ibid.

4 Ibid.

5 Ibid.

6 Ibid.

7 Ibid.

FANNIE MAE, FREDDIE MAC AND POLITICIANS AS EXPERTS ON THE ECONOMY

8   Liz Moyer, "After the Bailout," *Forbes.com,* September 8, 2008, available at http://www.forbes.com/2008/09/07/fannie-freddie-bailout-biz-wall-cx_im_fanniefreddie3_ ... (last visited September 25, 2008).

9   "All Recipients of Fannie Mae and Freddie Mac Campaign Contributions, 1989–2008," (September 18, 2008). Available at http://www.audacityofhypocrisy.com/2008/09/18/all-recipients-of-fannie-mae-and-freddie- ... (last visited September 24, 2008).

10 Luke Mullins, "Chris Dodd: Economy and Constitution at Risk," September 23, 2008, available at http://www.usnews.com/blogs/the-home-front/2008/09/23/chris-dodd-economy-and-consti ... (last visited September 24, 2008).

11 Ibid.

12 John T. Woolley & Gerhard Peters, "Statement on Signing the Housing and Community Development Act of 1992," *The American Presidency Project,* (October 28, 1992), available at http://www.presidency.ucsb.edu/ws/print.php?pid=21697 (last visited September 25, 2008).

13 Ibid.

14 Stephen LaBaton, "New Agency Proposed to Oversee Freddie Mac and Fannie Mae," *The New York Times,* September 11, 2003.

15 Ibid.

16 Ibid.

17 "Dodd Statement on Fannie Mae, Freddie Mac," July 13, 2008, available at http://dodd.senate.gov/index.php?q=node/4501/print (last visited September 25, 2008).

18 "Dodd Reacts to President's Address," September 24, 2008, available at http://dodd.senate.gov/index.php?q=node/4576/print (last visited September 25, 2008).

19 Michael Scherer, "House GOP Leaders Blame Pelosi's Statement," *Time*, September 29, 2008, available at http://www.time-blog.com/swampland/2008/09/house_leaders_blame_pelosis_st.html (last visited September 29, 2008).

20 "Prepared Remarks of President Barack Obama," *Financial Times*, February 25, 2009, available at http://www.ft.com/cms/s/bofea552–02df-11de-b58b-000077b07658, ... (last visited February 27, 2009).

POLITICAL DISCOURSE

21 "Constitution of the United States of America"

22 Ibid.

23 Ibid.

24 "Matthew Chapter 7," *The Holy Bible*.

25 "The Declaration of Independence of the United States of America."

TERROR ATTACK, WAR AND RESPONSIBILITY

26 "One Hundred Seventh Congress of the United States of America," *Senate Joint Resolution 45, Authorization for Use of Military Force*, September 26, 2002.

27 Ibid.

28 Ibid.

29 "One Hundred Seventh Congress of the United States of America," *Authorization of the Use of United States Armed Forces Against Iraq–Motion to Proceed,* October 3, 2002.

30 "Transcript for January 11th," *Meet The Press with Tim Russert,* January 11, 2004, available at http://msnbc.msn.com/id/3916793/ (last visited September 21, 2004).

31 "President Says Saddam Hussein Must Leave Iraq Within 48 Hours," *The White House, President George W. Bush, Office of the Press Secretary,* March 17, 2003 available at http://www.whitehouse.gov/news/releases/2003/03/20030317–7.html.

32 Ibid.

33 "Transcript for January 11th," *Meet the Press with Tim Russert,* January 11, 2004, available at http://msnbc.msn.com/id/3916793/ (last visited September 21, 2004).

34 Ibid.

35 Ibid.

36 "Congressional Approval Falls to Single Digits for First Time Ever," *Rasmussen Reports,* July 8, 2008, available at http://www.rasmussenreports.com/public_content/politics/mood_of_america/congressional... (last visited October 8, 2008).

FANNIE AND FREDDIE REVISITED; CHARACTER OF THOSE IN THE KNOW

37 Kathleen Day & Terence O'Hara, "False Signatures Aided Fannie Mae Bonuses, Falcon Says," *Washington Post,* April 7, 2005, available at http://www.washingtonpost.com/ac2/wp-dyn/A32845–2005Apr6?language=printer (last visited October 7, 2008).

38 Franklin D. Raines, "Don't Tar Us With an Enron Brush," *The Wall Street Journal,* February 25, 2002, available at http://online.wsj.com/article/SB1014596127135837040.html (last visited October 10, 2008).

39 The Associated Press, "Biden explains Indian-American remarks," *MSNBC,* July 7, 2006, available at http://www.msnbc.msn.com/id/13757367/print/1/displaymode/1098/ (last visited April 30, 2009).

POLITICIANS, PEOPLE, MEDIA, SOME ISSUES

40 David Espo, "Specter says he's switching from GOP to Democrats," *Yahoo! News,* April 28, 2009, available at http://www.yahoo.com/s/ap/20090428/ap_on_go_co/us_specter_switch/print (last visited April 28, 2009).

41 Chris Strohm, "Powell Says Shrinking GOP Should Return To The Center," *National Journal,* May 5, 2009, available at http://www.nationaljournal.com/congressdaily/print_friendly.php?ID=cda_20090505_8843 (last visited May 7, 2009).

42 "Congressman Says Western Pa. Was 'Really Redneck,'" *The Pittsburgh Channel. Com,* October 20, 2008, available at http://www.thepittsburghchannel.com/print/17764334/detail.html (last visited October 27, 2008).

43 "Pinocchio," *Walt Disney Home Video,* Distributed by Buena Vista Home Video, Dept. CS, Burbank, California 91521.

44 Lauren Stiller Rikleen, "Women need Katie Couric to succeed," September 4, 2006, available at http://www.scrippsnews.com/node/12290 (last visited March 5, 2009).

45 Ibid.

46 Ibid.

47 "Couric Gets Honored in D.C.," June 11, 2008, available at http://www.mediabistro.com/fishbowldc/television/couric_gets_honored_in_dc_86823.asp (last visited March 5, 2009).

48 "Excerpts: Charlie Gibson Interviews Sarah Palin," *ABC News*, September 11, 2008, available at http://abcnews.go.com/print?id=5782924 (last visited March 4, 2009).

49 Donna Brazile, "Anchor Aweigh: How Will History Sound in Katie Couric's voice?," fall 2006, available at http://msmagazine.com/fall2006/donnabrazile.asp (last visited March 4, 2009).

SOCIAL OBSERVATIONS

50 Donna Brazile, "Anchor Aweigh: How Will History Sound in Katie Couric's voice?," fall 2006, available at http://msmagazine.com/fall2006/donnabrazile.asp (last visited March 4, 2009).

51 Maureen Dowd, "The Tracks of Our Tears," *The New York Times*, November 9, 2008, available at http://www.nytimes.com/2008/11/09/opinion/09dowd.html?pagewanted=print (last visited November 12, 2008).

52 Ibid.

53 Michael Barone, "White House Census Power Grab May Violate the Constitution," *U.S. News & World Report*, February 9, 2009, available at http://www.usnews.com/blogs/barone/2009/02/09/white-house-census-power-grab-may-viol… (last visited May 2, 2009).

54 Clarence Thomas, *My Grandfather's Son*, HarperCollins Publishers, New York, 2007, pp. 74–75.

LIPS CAN STOP VERY LITTLE FOR GOOD OR ILL

55 "Bush Says it is Time For Action," November 6, 2001, available at http://cnn.allpolitics.printthis.clickability.com/pt/cpt?action=cpt&title=CNN.com+-+Bush+s ... (last visited May 4, 2009).

56 Philip Elliott, "Obama Announces Plan to Close Tax Loopholes," *Associated Press,* May 4, 2009, available at http://news.yahoo.com/s/ap/20090504/ap_on_bi_ge/us_obama_taxes/print (last visited May 4, 2009).

57 "Bush Says it is Time For Action," November 6, 2001, available at http://cnn.allpolitics.printthis.clickability.com/pt/cpt?action=cpt&title=CNN.com+-+Bush+s ... (last visited May 4, 2009).

GOVERNMENT BY LIBERALS, FOR LIBERALS

58 William J. Clinton, "Securing the Common Good: A Vision for America and the World," *Center for American Progress,* October 18, 2006, available at http://www.americanprogress.org/events/special_events/commongood_wjc.html (last visited December 4, 2008).

59 Ibid.

60 Ibid.

61 Clarence Thomas, *My Grandfather's Son,* HarperCollins Publishers, New York, 2007, p. 98.

62 William J. Clinton, "Securing the Common Good: A Vision for America and the World," *Center for American Progress,* October 18, 2006, available at http://www.americanprogress.org/events/special_events/commongood_wjc.html (last visited December 4, 2008).

63 Ibid.

FREEDOM AND ENGLISH

64 "The Declaration of Independence of the United States of America."

65 Ibid.

66 "Exodus Chapter 20," *The Holy Bible.*

67 "Couple: County Trying to Stop Home Bible Studies," 10 *News. Com,* May 25, 2009, available at http://www.10news.com/print/19562217/detail.html (last visited May 29, 2009).

68 "Exodus Chapter 20," *The Holy Bible.*

69 "Constitution of the United States of America," Amendment I.

70 "Gay NH Bishop to Offer Prayer at Inaugural Event," *The Associated Press,* January 12, 2009, available at http://news.yahoo.com/s/ap20091012/ap_on_re_us/gay_bishop_obama/print (last visited January 12, 2009).

71 "Former Rep. Bob Livingston on Sen. Dick Durbin's Controversial Remarks," *Fox News Hannity & Colmes,* June 20, 2005, available at http://www.foxnews.com/printer_friendly_story/0,3566,160106,00.html (last visited May 11, 2009).

72 Senator Reid on Iraq, "This War is Lost," *CBS/AP,* April 20, 2007, available at http://www.cbsnews.com/stories/2007/04/20/politics/main2709229.shtml (last visited May 11, 2009).

73 "Kerry Suggests Troops Lazy, Not Bright," *World Net Daily*, October 31, 2006, available at http://www.worldnetdaily. com/news/article.asp?ARTICLE_ID=52705 (last visited May 11, 2009).

74 Pauline W. Chen, M.D., "When the Patient Gets Lost in Translation," *The New York Times*, April 23, 2009, available at http://www.nytimes.com/2009/04/23/health/23chen. html?pagewanted=print (last visited June 9, 2009).

LIBERAL POLICIES, RACIAL CHALLENGES AND THE IMPORTANCE OF EDUCATION

75 "Rep. Frank Calls Scalia a 'Homophobe' in Interview," *The Associated Press*, March 23, 2009, available at http://abcnews. go.com/print?id=7154174 (last visited May 12, 2009).

76 Juan Williams, "Judge Obama on Performance Alone," *The Wall Street Journal*, January 20, 2009, available at http:// online.wsj.com/article/SB123249791178500439.html (last visited January 21, 2009).

77 Ibid.

78 "Text of Rev. Lowery's Inauguration Benediction," *The Associated Press*, January 20, 2009, available at http://news. yahoo.com/s/ap/20090120/ap_on_go_pr_wh/inauguration_ lowery_text/print (last visited January 21, 2009).

79 Rachel Potucek, "Affirmative Action: Pros and Cons," *K-State Perspectives*, fall 2003, available at http://www.k-state.edu/media/webzine/0203/aapros&cons.html (last visited November 13, 2008).

80 *Webster's II New College Dictionary, Houghton Mifflin Company*, copyright 2001, p. 333.

ROLE, PURPOSE, AND POWER OF GOVERNMENT

81 "Proverbs Chapter 29," *The Holy Bible.*

82 Philip Elliott, "Obama Touts Middle-Class Task Force Led by Biden," *The Associated Press,* January 30, 2009, available at http://news.yahoo.com/s/ap/20090130/ap_on_go_pr_wh/obama_labor/print (last visited January 30, 2009).

83 Ibid.

84 Ibid.

85 Ibid.

86 Ibid.

87 Ibid.

88 "First Inaugural Address," January 20, 1981, available at http://www.reaganlibrary.com/reagan/speeches/first.asp (last visited March 26, 2009).

89 Ibid.

90 Julie Hirschfeld Davis, "Pelosi Says Bush Team Misled Her on Waterboarding," *The Associated Press,* May 14, 2009, available at http://news.yahoo.com/s/ap/20090514/ap_on_go_co/us_pelosi_torture/print (last visited May 14, 2009).

91 "Rightwing Extremism: Current Economic and Political Climate Fueling Resurgence in Radicalization and Recruitment," *U.S. Department of Homeland Security, Office of Intelligence and Analysis Assessment,* April 7, 2009.

92 Ibid.

93 Ibid.

94 Ibid.

95 Ibid.

96 Ibid.

97 Ibid.

98 Ibid.

99 Ibid.

SUCCESS OR FAILURE

100 Bill Sammon, "Flashback: Carville Wanted Bush to Fail," *Fox News*, March 11, 2009, available at http://www.foxnews. com/politics/2009/03/11/carville-wanted-bush-fail/ (last visited March 11, 2009).

101 David A. Patten, "DNC Joins Anti-Limbaugh Crusade," *Newsmax*, March 5, 2009, available at http://www.newsmax. com/printTemplate.html. (last visited March 6, 2009).

102 Jeff Zeleny and John Harwood, "Obama Promises Bid to Overhaul Retiree Spending," *The New York Times*, January 8, 2009, available at http://www.nytimes.com/2009/01/08/us/politics/08obama.html?_r=1 &ref=health&pagewa ... (last visited March 11, 2009).

103 Philip Elliott, "Obama Touts Middle-Class Task Force Led by Biden," *The Associated Press*, January 30, 2009, available at http://news.yahoo.com/s/ap/20090130/ap_on_go_pr_wh/obama_labor/print (last visited January 30, 2009).

104 Liz Sidoti, "Obama: Get the Dread Out of Tax Deadline Day," *The Associated Press*, April 15, 2009, available at http://news.yahoo.com/s/sp/20090415/ap_on_go_pr_wh/obama/print (last visited April 15, 2009).

105 Matt Moon, "Special Report: How Do Americans Feel About Taxes Today?," *Tax Foundation*, April 2009, No. 166, available at http://www.taxfoundation.org/files/sr166.pdf (last visited April 21, 2009).

106 Liz Sidoti, "Obama: Get the Dread Out of Tax Deadline Day," *The Associated Press,* April 15, 2009, available at http://news.yahoo.com/s/sp/20090415/ap_on_go_pr_wh/obama/print (last visited April 15, 2009).

WAIT, WHAT?

107 Jim Meyers, "Democrats Look to Muzzle Conservative Radio," *Newsmax,* February 6, 2009, available at http://www.newsmax.com/printTemplate.html (last visited February 6, 2009).

108 Ibid.

109 Ibid.

110 Ibid.

111 Toby Harnden, "Barack Obama: 'Arrogant US Has Been Dismissive' to Allies," *Telegraph,* April 3, 2009, available at http://www.telegraph.co.uk/news/worldnews/northamerica/usa/barackobama/5100338/Bar ... (last visited April 18, 2009).

112 "The Declaration of Independence of the United States of America."

113 "My Country, 'Tis of Thee," Text: Samuel F. Smith, 1808–1895.